Changing Ideas
A story of a Muslim convert

Ian Nisbet

1st Edition

This book incorporates two previously published books: 'Why I became a Muslim' and 'Inside Mubarak's Prison.'

مكتبة اسلامية MaktabaIslamia

MaktabaIslamia Publications

www.maktabaislamia.com
info@maktabaislamia.com
www.facebook.com/everythingislamic
www.twitter.com/maktabaislamia

2016 CE – 1437 H

Translation of the Qur'ān

It should be perfectly clear that the Qur'ān is only authentic in its original language, Arabic. Since perfect translation of the Qur'ān is impossible, we have used the translation of the meaning of the Qur'ān throughout the book, as the result is only a crude meaning of the Arabic text.

Qur'ānic verses appear in speech marks proceeded by a reference to the Surah and verse number. Sayings (*Hadith*) of Prophet Muhammad ﷺ appear in inverted commas along with reference to the Hadith Book and its Reporter.

ﷺ - صلى الله عليه وسلم (Peace be upon him)
ﷻ - سبحانه وتعالى (Glory to Him, the Exalted)

Introduction

Most of the first part of this book was written while I was still in Mazra'a Tora prison in Cairo, Egypt. I have edited the content a little and added some more content (*italicised*), but otherwise it is as I wrote it in 2004. I wrote it for my son, as I had not seen him for one and a half years, had not yet been sentenced, and so I was unsure whether I would ever know him properly. I wrote this as an attempt to let him know me when he is grown up.

The manuscript was hand written on thin exercise book paper. I took about fifty sheets at a time, folded and put them in small plastic bags. I then put them under the insole of my shoes, so that when I was searched at the entrance to the visiting area, they would not be discovered. Finally, during the visit I would visit the bathroom, move the papers to my pocket and then pass them to my visitor who generally was not searched while leaving the prison. Over the course of a week my whole book was successfully smuggled out of the prison, then finally back to England where it waited for me to type it up when I returned in 2006.

I got stuck into the task about a month after I arrived, then I added a whole second section detailing my treatment at the hands of the Egyptian State Security and prison system. It was actually great therapy to put it all on paper, as some of the ordeal had been quite traumatic to talk about. I sought a publisher for the still unfinished book in 2007, but was told that there was no market for such a book, so it sat on the shelf for the next six years.

Finally, I decided to initially self publish the second part of my book, although still many stories of daily prison life have yet to be written. Here then, are both parts of my book, detailing my thinking and changes that ultimately led me to become a political prisoner, adopted by Amnesty International as a prisoner of conscience.

London   Ian Nisbet
June 2013

Contents

Part 1

My Early Life	11
My Attitude as a Teenager	14
Rap and Hip-Hop	18
Discovering Islam	22
Meeting a Muslim	25
I Wasn't Alone	29
Challenging My Thoughts	32
Belief in God	34
The Qur'an is God's Word	37
Islam and Science	40
Philosophies	46
Is European Culture Universal?	48
Freedoms	52
There is no Truth?	54
The Islamic Vision	56
Look What I Discovered!	60
Submission or Choice	62
Christian Belief and Contentment	66

Becoming a Muslim	71
Family Relationships	75
Changed Personality	77
Fate and Fatalism	83
Accessing Information about Islam	87
Carrying the *Da'awa* / Studying Arabic	95

Part 2

Egypt	103
Taken	107
Torture	111
Interrogation	117
Prosecutor	131
Prison	135
British Consul	138
Punishment Cells	140
Investigation	145
Charged	150
The Case Continues	152
The Courtroom	157
The Prosecution	164
The Defence	168

First Visit	171
The Sentence	173
Life inside the Prison	178
Prison History	184
Tensions	191
Punishment Cells	194
Released	200
Photos	204

As Salaamu Alaikum my dear son,

As I write this you are my first and only son, *Alhamdulillah*, whom I love dearly and ask Allah to grant the best of this life and the best of the next life. You are now four years old, but will be much older by the time that you read this.

Sadly, for the past twenty one months I have not been able to be with you and have seen you only briefly a handful of times. Allah knows what the future holds for us both, and how much of our lives can be spent in each other's company. I write for you the story of my life now so that you will always know your devoted and loving father, come what may. *Insha' Allah* (God willing), I will be given the strength to complete it, at least up until the current date and stage of my life at 29 years of age.

As you have been raised as a Muslim boy by your mother, a devoted and God fearing woman of whom only good words can be said, as I see it, you have not known any other way of life. You have not known the darkness of misguidance of which Allah speaks about many times in His Glorious book. You have never known me as anything other than as a Muslim, but I was not always like that. I only accepted Islam at the age of twenty, five years before you were born. At the time this was unusual, and I was the only convert to Islam that I actually knew.

Part 1

My Early Life

I was born in August 1974 in Cheltenham general hospital, I am told, on a Friday Morning at about 9am by caesarean section operation due to the doctor wanting to rush off to a golfing weekend that he had planned. We moved to Brackley when I was nearly five years old. I remember only a little of my early childhood. I remember having the mumps when I was three. I remember a toy rifle that fired plastic bullets. I remember my sandpit and the Bay tree in the Garden in which I could climb and then jump out of. I used to ride on my tractor and I had a Tonka tipper truck to push around. My best friend at the time was a neighbour whom I started school with. We rode the bus together with our sisters. I remember playing trains in the playground and I used to look across to the junior school and be amazed at how big everyone there was.

When we moved to Brackley, the housing estate was still being built so there was lots of mud to play with and make mud pies for my mum as gifts. On my fifth birthday I had a party and had some neighbours along who were of a similar age. One girl spilled her drink about three times and so I never really liked her. For a few years I was friends with two neighbourhood boys, but then drifted when I met Craig. He was my age and we were inseparable every day out of school for the next ten years. We finally drifted when I started at Nene College in Northampton at sixteen years old. We met occasionally after this, but hardly know each other now.

We mostly played with Lego, building camps in the fields behind our houses or riding bikes after I learned when I was about seven years old.

Craig's father was a motocross rider and so we sometimes went to watch races on Sundays. We would often ride our bikes on the neighbourhood paths, terrorising pedestrians. If anyone complained, we would shout out "it's a free country!" On Sundays when I didn't go, I used to spend my time with my next door neighbour Steven. We often ended up baking cakes to eat in his kitchen or mine. These skills have become useful while here in the prison.

Craig and I were never in the same classes at school so I spent my time with completely different friends. We had a group of about eight who spent most lessons together. I've almost lost touch with all of them now. Only one I met regularly after we both went to universities in London.

At junior school I acted in three school plays. "James and the giant peach" in which I was a wasp and a member of the crowd; "The Wizard of Oz" in which I was a brainless soldier of Oz; and in a third play I was an Italian pizza seller with a few lines to say. I learned to play piano for about six months, but lost interest in the classical tunes I was playing. I took art as an option at school, but never really accomplished much. I enjoyed copying existing artwork, but didn't like to create my own original work. I made my own comic once, but didn't get past the first issue. Craig, his brother Daniel and I created a pop group called CID (Craig, Ian and Daniel). We wrote about ten songs, performed them to our parents and were advised not to give up our day jobs. We had a guitar that we strummed tunelessly, an old toy organ and some suitcases for drums. We made a terrible noise. Aside from this I never got into 'the arts'.

While at school, I changed my life's ambition from wanting to be a train driver, which I took from my dad's love of all things steam, to wanting to be an architect, or a draftsman, or just a technical illustrator.

My favourite toy was Technical Lego and I loved, and still do, love all things technical. I made vending machines from shoe boxes, go-karts from wood and old prams, and tree houses from anything that I could find.

For GCSE Technology I made a "Record Flipper-Over" which almost worked, except that it wouldn't lift the Record high enough so would crash into the centre spindle and get stuck. I made a DJ Mixer with a three band panoramic equaliser while studying a BTEC National Diploma in Engineering at college in Northampton. This did work. I attempted a multiple input MIDI controller for electronic musical instruments for my final year degree project of a BEng Honours Degree in Computer and Control Engineering. This was only partially successful, but was awarded 2:1 grade, despite its short comings. As can be seen from most of my technical projects, I virtually lived for my music. I was mainly interested in Hip Hop music. I soon became obsessed with the technical side of electronic music production and DJ-ing. I even had a very brief job as a night club DJ while at university in London. The club closed down permanently soon afterwards.

When I was about eleven I got to hear songs on Top-of-the-Pops BBC TV programme by "Doug E Fresh", "the Fresh Prince" and "the Whistle" and I loved them. Then when I heard "Go see the Doctor" by "Kool Moe Dee" at a friend's house I became hooked on rap music.

My Attitude as a Teenager

At Sixteen I bought my first DJ turntable and slowly built a four track and then an eight track recording studio in my bedroom. As I moved house while a student, my recording equipment went with me. I spent around 4000 pounds on it which I had saved from jobs in the Odeon cinema in Streatham, Summer Factory work and various other part time work in shops, kitchens, waiting tables, delivering milk and so on. I was more or less addicted to buying records. If I had any spare money it would always be spent on a new record. I could hardly walk past a record store without making a new purchase. I collected about five hundred records in all.

The other drain on my student finances was the regular Friday and Saturday night drinking sessions with my friends. While I was seventeen I forged a college application form to make my age appear to be eighteen, thus obtaining a student union ID card by deception to allow me to buy alcohol while under age. As I never drove a car, I invariably got drunk almost every time we went out. Of course I became much more confident while intoxicated, as it allowed me to shed my inhibitions. I suspect that I even thought that I was more interesting to talk to as well.

I always loved my family very much, yet as I became a teenager I began to neglect them. I was more concerned with going out with my friends than to spend time with my parents, for example, so as a result, we began to become more distant. I realise now how hurtful it was for my parents to be treated like live-in-servants and not really know me, as I was always out of the house. At the time, it just seemed so normal to place my own desires so far above their feelings. Everyone else that I knew was doing the same. Some of my acquaintances even used to bad-mouth their parents behind their backs. I was never able to do that, as I didn't have any ill-feeling towards my parents, and I thought that it was a very disrespectful thing to do. I remember one time that some school friends made fun of my father's habit of taking obscure photographs of plant life for his camera club competition. I became embarrassed, but said nothing to them, as I feared that they'd laugh at me too.

I had always been dragged to church on Sunday mornings. Only once a month would I sit in with the congregation, while the rest of the time I would be in Sunday school learning about various Christian teachings about morality and beliefs. I must have enjoyed it at times, but when I was about eleven I stopped behaving myself and started to play up the teachers and behave silly. I didn't really find the moral teachings very interesting and I had stopped to believe any of it was true. None of my friends went to church, and although I wasn't mocked for my own attendance, I did feel it was un-cool to go, so kept it a secret as much as possible. I was also with the cub scouts and started to misbehave in the same way until I was eventually asked to leave. My wrists were actually tied with rope to the rafters of the scout hut, as I refused to take my hands out of my pockets while standing to attention. I then joined the scouts for a while but got bored of that too. I reckon that I was a very average person at that age and my attitude was similar to that of my peers. We were, basically, all very self centred people.

At the age of fourteen I had a milk delivery job before school and on Saturdays, so I could afford to buy records occasionally. I started to buy more and more records and became very impressed with newer and cleverer rhymes. I soon started to prefer the more conscious raps that attempted to tackle serious subjects. These were always more interesting than yet another rhyme about how amazing such and such rapper is.

Accompanying this music was a magazine called "Hip-Hop Connection" which allowed rappers to expand on their views in interviews. Hence, I started to hear views and opinions of American and British predominantly men in their twenties, usually complaining about their societal circumstances, racism, poverty, police brutality, slavery and religion, which became familiar themes, so I was awoken to the existence of a complex world with some acute societal problems, both historically and still existing today. This awareness led to feelings of disgust for the status-quo, as I started to care about the plight of others.

I began to consider seriously the issues mentioned and made myself aware of wider political issues such as war and the environment. I got an A at GCSE Geography because the exam questions were about environmental issues and recycling, which I was already passionate about. The BBC started a series of documentaries about the American civil rights movement and so I took a lot of interest in this, as many of the main names involved were often mentioned as folk heroes in rap music. I became aware of the passive struggle approach to change as favoured by the NAACP and Martin Luther King. It basically entailed working to reform the current system from within the system. I contrasted this to the radical approach which favours starting afresh, getting rid of the whole old system and replacing it with a new one: not gradually but radically. The second approach was the way of Malcolm X and was anything but Christian or tolerant.

When I was seventeen, I had begun to view anything to do with Western governments as inherently bad and selfish, rife with corruption and injustices due to discrimination and exploitation. So when the UN coalition forces invaded Iraq in the 1991 war, I felt that it was unjust and that Saddam must have been the oppressed one, simply because it was Bush and Major rallying against him.

I was very much affected by the film "Cry Freedom" (1987) about the life and death of the black South African freedom fighter Steven Biko. I was growing up during the end of the Apartheid years and school projects involved becoming more aware of the oppression overseas. I was ashamed, as were many other English folk, that Margaret Thatcher would not even introduce a trade embargo against De-Clerk. I refused to eat South African fruit at the time.

Rap and Hip-Hop

Through rap music and the likes of KRS-One, Public Enemy, Paris, the Poor Righteous Teachers, X-Clan, and the Last Poets I discovered, first, Malcolm X and then the Socialist Black Panthers. While I was in my first year at university, I read the autobiographies of Malcolm X and Bobby Seale, who was the co-founder of the Black Panther party in 1960s Oakland California. I was living in the University of Westminster halls of residence in Streatham in London. I was introduced to a whole new perspective on life.

Much of the thinking in Malcolm X's book appears throughout late 1980s early 1990s rap music. Others had built upon this to come up with new philosophies of life and some poignant lyrics that served as food for thought for me.

Growing up, I effectively rejected the church from the age of about 13. I saw no relevance in its teachings to my life. I had serious doubts about the authenticity of the Bible and even the existence of God. I started to give it no importance and so ignored the question entirely. However, it was my favourite rappers that started me thinking about it again. Religion and politics were hot topics between 1987 and 1994 in the world of Hip-Hop. The NWA style Gansta Rap that started around 1989 was still growing and older political rap was struggling against it and its negative messages. I stopped following rap music in December 1994, but I learned later that political rap almost died after that and Gansta rap became the new pop music. Only after 9-11-2001, I hear, did political rap start to make waves again.

Below are the lyrics from one example that had a meaning for me:

Emancipation is long overdue,
So overcome procrastination, because freedom is within you

For some reason we think we're free,
So we'll never be, because we haven't recognised slavery...

Where is our God, the God that represents us?
The God that looks like me, the God that I can trust?
A God of peace and love, not mass hysteria,
I don't want a God that blesses America,
I could never really vote for the devil,
Let me take you to a higher level...

Like liquor, we are God-Intoxicated,
Not to the true God, but the one the government created,
The same governments telling people to vote,
I pray to God because the people have lost hope,
You either vote for the mumps or the measles,
Whether you vote for the lesser of two evils, you vote for evil

Politics and God are not equal,
But the education if you don't guard, is really lethal...

Rap music is such an influential art form, because it allows the artist to express himself in quite considerable detail. Rappers can talk at length about their ideas. Yet, it is a rhythmic composition so it has a catchiness to it that allows one to repeat it over and over and so the ideas expressed become more and more familiar to the listener. A book is rarely read over and over, but poetry is, and it is memorised too. So, by repeatedly hearing the same thought expressed, usually when alone or on a journey, allows one plenty of time to contemplate what is being said. It is the contemplation that is important.

One of the main points that I took from my reading and listening was that God had a way for us to live, but that people had corrupted the revelations and had added superstitions to religion. I also saw that political problems can be solved by employing political solutions, which is what the Black Panthers were all about. I never really got into the socialist philosophies of the Black Panthers, as I had started to consider that God may exist after all.

I began to wonder why people accepted the existence of racism and oppression in their societies. I concluded that a lot of people in Britain and America just follow the crowd with very few people actually thinking about such problems and becoming leaders among them. So, with mass ignorance and insincere leaders, cynically using their positions for personal benefits, such problems become ingrained in the culture. Thus, I considered that the solution lay in replacing the insincere thought leaders with sincere ones; hence, I would need to become educated, trusted and then influential myself. But, I couldn't see any reason why people should accept my ideas over another's, so I became stuck. Should we adopt whatever is said, just because the respected rapper said it? This may well be true for many youth, or even the many adults who adopt the point of view expressed by newspaper journalists or TV broadcasters, however adopting ideas based upon respect for the one expressing those ideas is so dangerous, yet sadly so common. Rather, contemplating the idea and adopting it based upon its merits is far more suitable for intelligent human beings.

I had a very humanitarian and liberal view on the world at the time, which was focused on removing suffering and injustices such as racism, poverty, oppression etc. I felt that oppression and oppressors are evil and must be stopped by whatever means. The big problem for me was "what should it all be replaced with?" It's not unusual to meet people who sense problems in the world and want to make some changes "to make the world a better place". Such feelings had developed gradually in me throughout the years that I was growing up hearing rappers list societal problems in their music, but it is one thing to feel the existence of problems, and quite another thing to know the solution.

After some agonizing and frustration over issues like this during my second year at university I decided to take a year away from my studies to pursue my music production ambitions and, more importantly, to spend some time in the library searching for answers to my many questions. There was no world wide web to speak of in 1994.

Discovering Islam

I had come to understand from Malcolm X that a Muslim is one who submits to Allah, so I respected this. I was sure that Allah, as the Creator, must have sent a clear system for solving such societal problems, but I didn't know what it was.

I wasn't thinking a lot about life and death and what happens after death at this time. I generally avoided such thoughts, as they were a dead-end for me; I had no answers. However, at this time I went on a package holiday with my friends to Majorca and while on the plane I started to feel anxious and afraid, suddenly aware of my mortality, so I prayed to myself that if I die I wanted to die as a Muslim, someone who submitted himself to Allah. I still knew almost nothing about Islam at this time. I knew that Allah was synonymous with God, the Creator. I knew that the Jews had the Torah, the Christians had the Bible and that Muslims had the Qur'an, and that all claimed to have been sent by the same God, Allah. I wasn't confused with using the name Allah for God, as I knew that it was just and Arabic name meaning "the God", as opposed to "a god" which carries the implication of many gods, but Allah carries the meaning of a supreme God, which is what we mean in English when we say God with a capital "G".

Soon after I returned from my holiday I watched on TV the film "The Ten Commandments" with Charlton Heston in it as Moses. I was suddenly struck with the thought that Allah had revealed laws for mankind and I was brought to tears at the end of the film. I felt that now I must search through the Torah, the Bible and the Qur'an to find out what that revealed law was and to separate it from the man-made innovations that had crept into these books over time. It was exactly the answer that I needed, as now I knew that if I could encourage people to change their societies for the better, with the laws of Allah, then people would surely see a reason to follow and then we could solve our problems together. I went immediately to my bedroom to read from a Bible that an English teacher at school and a family friend had given to me years before, but which I had never really read. It was just the New Testament so I read from the chapter called Revelations and became very afraid of the prophesies within it and the prospect of death.

I had only one source of information about Islam at the time. At the "Fresher's Fair" in the university I had picked up some leaflets from the Student Union "Islamic Society" and had kept them. One was entitled "Democracy is Hypocrisy" and the other "The *Munkar* (Evil)". What I gained from them was that Islam had a comment about politics and offered some solutions.

I knew that I wasn't going to find many answers in my home town, so I moved to a dank bed-sit in Streatham, South London and returned to the Cinema for full-time work.

I went to the local library for books about Islam. I found one about smoking and its harm, and one was a refutation of many erroneous ideas held in Britain about Islam. It discussed such subjects as the Islamic *shari'ah* punishments, women's rights, slavery and other common slanders against Islam found in many Western writings. I took it home and was surprised by what I had found. I discovered that the whole of Islam, from ritual worships to social and political issues, was all legislation revealed by Allah to mankind. I also discovered that Islam is a completion of the previous revelations, an abrogation for the ways of the Torah and the Bible and was the final revelation to mankind. What had started as a convenient place to start looking soon became my main area of interest. I had basically discovered what I was looking for, so now I had a whole load of new questions.

Coincidently, at the same time I noticed a shop near to my house which had two books in the window. One, entitled "Jesus - the Prophet of Islam", and the second "Introduction to Islam" by Muhammad Hamidullah. It was the first time I'd heard Jesus described as a prophet and not the son of God. It seemed so much more sensible to me. I bought the second book.

Meeting a Muslim

At the same time, I attended a lecture organised by the socialist "Panther" party at my university. They had invited two Los Angeles gangsters, a Blood and a Crip, to talk about the current gang truce and black unity that the LA riots had spurned. I left the lecture feeling that I had learned very little in terms of a solution; I was even made to feel that my presence, as a white man, was not welcome; that I could not be part of their solution. On the way out a Muslim was distributing a leaflet about unity. It was a leaflet that he had written that day, as he knew that the Panther talk was due to happen that evening. I read his leaflet and then asked him if he was a Muslim, to which he replied that he was. At that moment I was very happy to meet him as I finally had found someone who could answer my questions about Islam, and moreover, he was actually inviting people to Islam and at the same time criticizing aspects of Western culture, which showed me that he had sensed a similar problem to what I had sensed and he was also presenting a solution.

The basic point of the leaflet was that any kind of unity, if it isn't based upon a belief that is convincing and at the same time provides solutions to life's problems, will be temporary and will be more divisive than unifying. The belief which is suitable for unifying human societies should be comprehensive, in that it addresses basic questions about life and that it gives complete solutions to human problems and a way to make these solutions exist in reality. Hence, the only real bond suitable for unifying people in all of their life's affairs is a comprehensive ideology. This is why the capitalist West works as well as it does, because the people are unified on a fundamental idea which gives them solutions to their daily problems. Islam, likewise, has solutions to daily problems and of course has a convincing fundamental belief. Bonds of a purely spiritual nature, nationalistic, racial, territorial bonds or bonds based solely upon common interests will not be sustainable and will fall apart and create disunity ultimately. The leaflet then pointed out that Islam is the only correct ideology.

It was a highly appropriate leaflet for the occasion of the Panther talk, as the speakers were encouraging black-unity against white oppression, as a replacement for black gang unity against other black gangs. In other words, they had just a reactionary, temporary solution to a much bigger problem. This was the central racialist discovery of the speakers, but was not the main aim of the talk organisers. They were an organisation called Panther which implied that they were an offshoot of the "Black Panther Party" of 1960s Oakland California. I had read the autobiography of one of the founders, Bobby Seale, called "Seize the time". They had proposed basic Socialist policies as a solution for black poverty and discrimination in America. The modern Panther group appeared to more like the "Socialist Workers Party" with a call to black and Asian unity as a front to introducing socialist ideas. I wasn't made to feel very welcome at the talk by one of the organisers. Being white, it was a unity that I could never partake in. On the other hand, the Muslim outside with his leaflet was proposing a completely different basis of unity which all people could partake in. Instead of adopting a temporary "all-of-the-down-trodden-against-the-common-enemy" reactionary approach, which will inevitably fizzle out once the enemy is subdued; the Islamic approach is to build a complete society based upon a common belief from which all solutions emanate. Hence, it is a permanent and practical unity which remains as long as that belief is actually referred to for all solutions. If that referring stops, then the belief is no longer the basis of the unity, and common interests take over that role. The biggest difference between the two solutions proposed that night is that the racial unity does not have inherent solutions to human problems, whereas the Islamic unity does.

This was exactly what I had been looking for and I recognised it immediately. I spent about an hour talking with Farhan, the Muslim leaflet distributor, then exchanged phone numbers agreeing to meet again for more discussion. When I went home I was so excited, as I had heard such wonderful news. I had learned that Islam was revealed to the prophet Muhammad (*May the blessings and peace of Allah be upon him*) as a complete way of life to solve all economic, political, social and religious problems for all of mankind. It does not differentiate between people other than how committed a person was in following Islam. Furthermore, all people, regardless of colour, religion, land of origin or gender are treated equally in front of the law. It does not have a special clergy or clerical class invested with the exclusive power to interpret Islamic texts and legislate accordingly; rather the texts are clear in the language of Arabic and open to all who want to read from them. Wherever there is ambiguity on a legal issue, then all people have the right to exercise their own effort to interpret the text according to their own conviction. I found that Islam is not a mere religion that only calls people to spiritual beliefs, but that it is the completion of the previous revealed religions and provides a complete political and spiritual belief for the modern times. All other religions had either been abrogated or proven false with the advent of Islam. I concluded that Islam is not merely a collection of political theories, but that it is a revealed way of life from the Creator of man, life and the universe, and that we owe it to our creator to be grateful for such a mercy and to worship him according to the manner of his choosing, which is to follow the Islamic way of life.

This was quite a discovery for me that day. I knew that my life was now about to change and that I had found a source of knowledge from where I could get my questions answered. I discovered that all of my anxiety and questioning was not unique to me. I didn't feel alone anymore in the world as at last I had found someone whom I could relate to and who could understand what was on my mind.

I Wasn't Alone

So confused and frustrated had I been prior to that meeting that I doubted if I could ever find someone to share my ideas and concerns with. I occasionally had tried to discuss some ideas with my friends, but no one really seemed willing to go further and most just preferred superficial discussions. At college I had a friend Tom, who hated racism as I did, but we never really discussed solutions. *I suspect that often we consider that just becoming a better individual will help make the society a better place. We rarely see the solution as involving political work; almost as if politics has no role in the makeup of society and its problems.*

My friends who listened to the same political rap songs were not as provoked into thought as I was, but were more into the music itself and the image, soon becoming bored of the politics. I once challenged a friend who was railing on about "Pakis", so I asked him what he meant by Paki, so he replied mockingly "smelly Indians". I shut up, as I had no convincing arguments to counteract with. My dislike of the unfairness and stupidity of racism had built up over years and I could not give precise reasons for my gut feelings that had developed over that time.

I tried to have meaningful conversations with another friend David, while we were both drunk. Intellectually he was really up for the challenge, but his heart wasn't in it. It was just the alcohol that opened him up to discussion.

I had tried to explain the injustices that I had noticed with family members. I pointed out that while we are all victims, our passiveness to such problems meant that we all share in responsibility too. One person close to me thought that I was blaming them and so became upset. I couldn't articulate my ideas very well at the time and I felt very bad that I had hurt someone I loved. My anger was for the system that allowed injustices to exist, not for all the individuals in the society, but I didn't express this very well. After this I stopped trying to explain my thoughts to people, so I felt alone in this matter. Just before I attended the Panther meeting I had already arrived at a point where I knew that I had to confront my worries though, or else I could never find the truth I was searching for.

A friend at the time who I trusted was a girl that I worked with at the cinema. One evening I just decided to pour all of my thoughts out. She was very polite in listening to me and agreed with some of what I was saying, but I sensed that it was all too heavy for her and that she was surprised that I had hidden so much away.

I later realised that there are people who give thought to political and social problems and do care about finding real solutions, but I just hadn't met them yet. If I had, then they kept it well hidden from me, just as I had hidden my own self. Possibly for the same reasons: incomplete solutions, confusion and fear of being ridiculed. The early 1990s for a teenager were all about partying and certainly not about political debate. Politics in universities had died off years before with most Student Union societies now geared towards sports and partying. Discussions about politics didn't seem to go much beyond a cynical disdain for the current state of affairs, but rarely involved discussion about solutions. People had resigned themselves to passive observation and so were decidedly depoliticised.

When I finally met Farhan, the Muslim with the leaflet, I was overwhelmed with happiness that other people were also troubled enough to look for real solutions, and even to invite others to consider them as well.

Challenging My Thoughts

That evening in October 1994, when I was twenty years old, began five weeks of self-reflection and changes that I could not have imagined just a short time earlier. I had already adopted a kind of morality, but it wasn't very firm. I had begun to consider my binge drinking as a frivolous waste of time, but I still enjoyed doing it. I had started to consider casual relationships with no commitment or responsibility as immoral, but I still had contradicting desires.

The problem for me was that I was torn between ideas about freedom and responsibility, which are of course contradictory. My morals had little basis other than gut feelings; not a very intellectual or convincing basis, so were often ineffective in restraining me. I would party hard, and then feel guilty afterwards.

Then came Farhan, who started to explain the intellectual basis of Islam; how all of the morals, rules and rituals can be traced back to the belief which is itself rationally based. The problem that I had with too much freedom, I found expression for. As I had long suspected, I heard that Allah had created us for a purpose and that he had revealed to us a set of values and laws to live life according to. So whilst Allah gave us a free ability to choose, it is a test for us whether we choose to do what Allah is pleased with and reject what Allah does not want us to do. This is a radically different viewpoint on life for an average English twenty year old. My viewpoint, and that of the society that produced me, had always been based upon the belief that each individual is completely free to choose; whether that be his religion, what to say, what to do or how to earn and spend his wealth. All of our problems can be solved by compromises, usually based upon the majority view. We rejected all notions of right or wrong and considered that there only existed shades of different opinions and that right and wrong are all relative to the individual. Whether we put this set of ideas into a moral framework was irrelevant. We all accepted this viewpoint on life as unquestionably superior. I just absorbed it from my environment, as it was reflected in every aspect of daily life and was the only viewpoint on offer in any case. When one's viewpoint is unquestionably superior, one tends not to have much debate about possible alternatives.

To challenge these "home-truths" with the idea that we are actually created to be slaves to our creator and not to be completely free; or that truth does exist and so does falsehood; or that compromise is not a suitable solution to all problems as Allah has defined for us what is good and what is bad and that we are only required to limit ourselves accordingly; all of this is a radically different approach to viewing life. This fact was not lost on me, nor was the beautiful simplicity of it all.

Belief in God

However, it is one thing to be impressed by a new idea, but it is quite another thing to believe that it is correct, absolutely. Farhan was aware of this so when I next arranged to meet with him, he gave me a booklet called "Faith and Progress" written by a convert to Islam. The booklet demonstrates in a methodical way how a person can rationally come to recognise that Allah's existence is a true fact and that the Qur'an is truly Allah's word.

Building upon rational concepts that the mind has established as fact we can determine that our existence and the existence of the universe necessitates Allah's existence. In other words, that we cannot possibly exist without Allah also existing.

I had been to Church and Sunday school for most of my life and I had asked how can we prove whether God exists or not? But I was never given a real answer. So, I came to reject belief in God for a while. I had been taught about a boy who asked his father "How can I know that God exists, but I can't see him?" To this the boy's father replied "If you taste salty water you know that the salt is there but you can't see it either." This, to me, is a poor analogy. Taste is a sense just like seeing is, and the salt is only dissolved in the water so is still sensible. The approach for Christians seemed to be: you can't really prove it, but it feels about right, so just take a leap of faith. I initially rejected this leap, but later felt it safer to sit on the fence and not be atheist; not denying God but instead thinking "If God exists…"

The approach for Muslims is entirely different, and this is what I discovered from the booklet and my continuing discussions with Farhan and now some friends of his with the Student Union Islamic Society at the university. A more suitable reply to the boy's question would be to say "when you taste water from a glass but didn't see anyone pour the water into the glass, you still know certainly that someone must have done so". Or another analogy is "when you meet a new adult, even though you didn't see him yesterday, you still know certainly that he existed yesterday. Rationally you know that for him to be a grown up and alive today, he must have been alive the day before as well." So the point is built upon a rational concept that every effect has a cause. This is a concept that we have built through interaction with our environment and has become a solid rational fact for us; only philosophers questions such rational facts, but as their thoughts are not constrained by reality, then they have no value in this discussion. *The point of such discussion is to understand our reality, after all.*

It is a rationally proven fact that we will all die at some time too; therefore our lives are limited by death. All things that can be sensed, i.e. our entire reality, are made up of things which are limited and dependent. They are dependent on things or on laws that define them. Nothing can be imagined by our limited minds except that we have some previous experience of it or what is similar to it. For example; no one can imagine what a new colour, that doesn't exist, can look like. What we end up imagining is just a mixture of what we have already previously sensed. All of this just demonstrates the limited nature of our reality.

Limited and dependent things don't exist by themselves, but depend upon something else also existing. This chain of dependency can be traced back, but ultimately it must end with something that is neither limited nor dependent. This entity is what Arab thinkers used to call *"wajid al-wujood"* (the obligatory that it exists). The one unlimited and independent entity is

Allah, *al-Awal* (the First), *al-Aakhir* (the Last), *as-Samad* (the everlasting), *ar-Raaziq* (the Sustainer) and *al-Khaaliq* (the Creator). These are a few of the names that Allah has given himself and that are mentioned in the Qur'an. It is this entity, Allah that Muslims refer all worship to, as it is only Allah that deserves gratitude for all that He has already given us, and none other deserves any worship except him, to whom belongs all praise.

If we clear our minds of prejudices and clearly ponder on the creation of all reality, then arriving at the above conclusion is inevitable. I did this and was shocked by the profoundness and simplicity of such a thought. It is the truth and I knew it, so now there was no running away from it. To have such a truth handed to me, to accept or to reject, I would have been a fool to reject it. I had shied from controversy my whole life, but this time the truth could not be denied. I believed it the first time I heard it. I still believe it now and *Insha'Allah* (God willing), I will die believing it. I knew that belief in God was not exactly popular in Britain, but this was the truth and I just had to accept it.

The Qur'an is God's Word

I had been reading from various books and a magazine called 'Al-Khilafah Magazine' along with leaflets that other Muslims gave to me. A friend of Farhan's called Asam, who was the president of the Student Union Islamic Society, spent a lot of time with me and we discussed the revelation of the Qur'an, the Prophet Muhammad and Islam.

We discussed how the Qur'an challenges those who doubt in its authenticity to produce a chapter like it. This challenge was for all Arabs at the time and for all who come after it. No one was able to do so, and until today that remains the case. This fact alone serves as a clear proof that the Qur'an is the authentic word of Allah. If the best of Arabs could not do so, then what hope is there for anyone else? Furthermore, anyone who actually takes time to read and study the Qur'an, with an open mind, will quickly realise its authenticity through countless evidences.

One fact that struck me is that Islam is the only religion that calls upon man to worship the creator alone. All other religions that I am aware of are actually encouraging people to worship what is created, whether idols, people, ideas etc. When this is considered alongside the abundant information contained in the Qur'an about the natural world, which modern science is only just starting to discover, then one realises that it is no forgery and is truly authentic.

I noticed that all other ideologies or political theories such as secularism, capitalism, socialism etc. were all originally a reaction to what existed before them. The oppression of the European kings and churches gave rise to secularism, separating church from state and promising previously denied freedoms, hence capitalism was born as a reaction. Marx's theories were all reactions to the capitalism that existed in Europe in his time. Yet Islam offers complete and balanced solutions to man's problems that address his real nature. They were not born out of a reaction to the problems facing the Arabs at the time. The other ideologies have developed over many years, with constant refinements, through trial and error. Islam was revealed to one man without any previous experience and did not go through a period of experimentation until it developed. The beginning of the revelation is entirely consistent with the end. So, there were no revisions or amendments that we see them in modern states' legislation today.

The Prophet Muhammad did not declare a law, which was then applied, but after some time was found to be flawed and so needed to be replaced or amended. This did not happen at all over the 23 year period in which the Qur'an was revealed. A small number of rules were abrogated by later rules, but these changes are not of the nature described here, which is so common in modern legislature. Many of the rights and theories, whether political, economic or social, that secular societies are only recently discovering in reaction to their experiences and mistakes of the past, already existed in Islam when it was revealed fourteen hundred years ago to Arabs who had nothing going for them prior to this, other than their literary heritage. Some ignorant Western folk think that they invented women's rights, emancipation of the slaves, innocent until proven guilty, political rights, accountability of rulers, elections, representative government, the rule of law, the right to life, religious tolerance, marketplace competition and so on. These are today hailed as the exclusive fruits of the European 'enlightenment', yet they all existed in Islam over fourteen centuries ago as part of a complete system of life which is not filled with contradictions or undergoing constant changes as people become "more enlightened".

How often do we admit past blatant injustices as "mistakes of the past" which "we have learnt from" and can "never happen again", sometimes just a decade ago? The European Convention on Human Rights which was recently adopted into the British legislature has had a huge impact on the criminal justice system here, where every day a new contradiction or problem occurs due to the generality of the human rights act and also the differing and changing interests in the society; a balance has yet to be found. We British have long prided ourselves on the 'Magna Carta', which gave rise to the principle of *habeas corpus*. Yet, today the British government is trying to take that right away from the people for a perceived benefit to their security. Islam was fixed at the time of revelation and has remained relevant and suitable for solving human problems through its application ever since. Modern British culture is a sadly lacking, "new kid on the block" in comparison. I recognised all of this as true, so how can Islam not come from Allah?

Islam and Science

It is often claimed that religion is irrational and contradicts science. I had always accepted this as a fact myself at face value without any further examination. I visited a natural history Museum, the Horniman, in South London close to where I was living during my second year of University. After seeing the skeletons of various animals I tended to agree with the conclusions of the curator; that humans had evolved from animals. To make such a shallow conclusion didn't take much thought; rather I just looked at the number of digits in a horse's foot and compared it to a human skeleton.

While working at the cinema the following year a colleague, who was a practicing Christian, lent me a book called "A bone of contention" *by Sylvia Baker*. The author is a Christian scientist who rejected evolutionary theory as improbable at best. This was the first time that I questioned it myself. Suddenly for me, just noticing a pattern in the similarities between us and animals was not such a conclusive proof of our evolution, but rather an indication of a common origin, which is a single creator.

None of this became solid until I was directed in my thoughts, by the Muslim's magazines and my new Muslim friends, to consider the very basis of thought itself.
Rational concepts are those that are built upon the mind. They are concepts which the mind confirms to be factual, such as "compromise between two opposites is impossible" hence a light is either on or off, but can never be in-between. Also, "every effect has a cause" is a rational concept for which the mind does not find any exceptions. These are conclusions based upon our experiences and are confirmed to be unchangingly true. Science is built upon this rational thought but it is a

branch of it and not rational of its own right. Science is based upon measurement and observation and then thinking of a theory to explain the observations. This theory could be right or wrong, accurate or inaccurate. A scientific theory can never cease to be a theory and should never be called a fact.

Science is useful as a tool to take benefit from our surroundings as it produces beneficial results when confined to its correct scope. It should not, however, be used outside of its scope. For example, the fossils in the earth and the rock layers show us that they were produced gradually over time. Scientists have sought to explain details of this process and exactly how these layers were produced, but they could be right or wrong. There really isn't a way to be precise when talking about the details of the past in this way, with so little evidence, so the scientific theory is an educated guess, but not a fact.

Due to the common history of oppression by the churches, science experienced an explosion of interest during the European 'enlightenment' years. Much of the Christian religious dogma came into question when it contradicted what the scientists rationally observed and their scientific theories. Ultimately, religion became discredited in Europe. It should be noted however that Islam never dissuaded science or discovery and that it positively thrived from the earliest days under Islamic rule. It was an exclusively European Christian phenomenon to keep the laymen ignorant in order to maintain church control. The current great love for science and hatred for religion in Britain is itself a reaction to this exclusively European history. Everything science nowadays is treated with utmost respect and blind following, whereas all religious ideas are shunned and accused of being reactionary. Science itself has become the new unquestionable dogma. It is just like the pot calling the kettle black. Muslims have never had the same problems that the European Christians had. For us, there is no contradiction between the natural world and the revelations of the Qur'an or the sayings of the Prophet, as they all come from the same source. Because we rationally proved that the Qur'an is the word of Allah and that Muhammad (*May the blessings and peace of Allah be upon him*) is his messenger, then what is contained within these two sources is the truth. The Qur'an talks of creating mankind from a single *nafs* (soul/self) so we accept this as a fact and need not question it further. A scientific theory, to stand any chance of being correct, must take this fact into consideration. *If a scientist developed a theory that we originated from more than one nafs, then it is clearly in error and must be rejected.* It would be ludicrous for us to accept some facts and reject others just because it contradicts our theories. This is dishonesty and it is far better for a scientist to admit that he doesn't really understand an exact process rather than to claim that he does while covering over certain problematic information.

Truthfully, there are no contradictions between what can be rationally observed of the natural world and what the Qur'an says of Allah's creation. The contradictions only appear between the Qur'an and some scientists' theories, when they claim, for example, that Allah does not exist. Clearly, those theories are incorrect as they are originally speculative, whereas the Qur'an is all true, rationally proven.

A scientist would be laughed at if he speculated a theory that airplanes cannot fly upside-down as it can be observed that planes do indeed fly upside-down. Yet, many from the scientific community do not laugh when he makes a statement that contradicts the Qur'an. This is a double standard. I read recently in a national newspaper an example of the shape of an airplane's wing, which is often said to be the cause of its lift, due to the curved top and the flat bottom. Rationally, we can see that lift occurs, but scientific theories that try to explain it are less certain. Some say that the shape alone creates the lift effect because the air on the top of the wing has to move faster than the air underneath, as it has a greater distance to travel. Hence, a pressure difference is created and lift occurs. Accordingly, flying upside down with the wing reversed would only generate downward "lift", so it would be impossible for the plane to stay in the air. Only a fool would cling to this logic and continue to say that a plane can't fly upside down after it was rationally observed.

Other scientists have other theories about the lift phenomenon; some may be right and others may be wrong, or maybe a mixture of both. But none of them change the reality and all of them are originally speculative attempts to explain what is rationally observed.

Human thought is a process that uses the brain. It is the connection of a sensed reality to some previous information which produces a judgment upon that reality. This is what a new thought is. This is the rational process and is the basis of all thoughts for all people. Scientific thought is a method of drawing conclusions based upon this, but is a branch of it and not the basis itself.

When a plane flies and it is observed by a person, he rationally judges it to be flying through the air. It is a fact which is not subjective, as long as that person has some previous information about the earth and the air etc. thus, a person can take measurements based upon this rational observation and can then think of theories to try to explain how the plane is flying. All of these theories are not facts, just theories. Even after a person produces experiments to test the theory, and then reaches a high degree of confidence in it, it still remains a theory. Rational observations are not theories though. Hence, as long as a theory remains a theory, then it is speculative and not certain.

An example of exaggerating the status of a theory is that for years Einstein's theory of relativity and the theories of thermodynamics were considered as facts by the scientific community, until quantum physics was investigated and the rules had to be redefined. The old rules were found not to work outside of certain limits, which had previously gone untested. If we have a known input into a box and we observe the output from the box, then we can make an estimate about the process inside it. We can produce a theory based upon experimentation and measurements taken from the inputs and outputs. This theory may "work" predictably for us and so we then have trust in it and assume that it works uniformly for all other inputs, not just the measured ones. However, it cannot become a fact until we actually take the lid off of the box and confirm rationally what the process is. What we observe can then be a rationally based fact for us. It is then built upon the mind, which itself is rational.

I'm not trying to imply here the commonly held notion that "you have to see it to believe it", which means that we can only believe what can be directly sensed. Based upon this notion some people jump to the conclusion that as we can't see or sense Allah, the Creator, directly so he must not exist. The mind is limited in its ability to make judgments only upon reality, therefore it cannot judge upon anything that has never been sensed. However, the mind is the suitable tool to judge the origin of the universe, as we can sense it. We can then judge that its origin must be unlike its nature which is limited and dependent, so its originator must be unlimited and independent. This is a rational judgment of the reality and does not involve scientific theorizing. The universe, man and life exist, so they must have an origin, a cause. As they are all limited and dependent, then the origin cannot be like them in this regard, so must be different.

But this is where we have to stop, as the mind is not able to further make judgments upon what it cannot sense. We judge only that there is a need for a Creator to exist before we can exist. We know Allah is there by implication not by direct sensation. So we cannot judge upon Allah's essence and nature, we must await revelation from Him to us, and then we say of Allah whatever Allah says He is.

During the days after I had first met Farhan I was developing a new way of thinking. Instead of blindly trusting whatever scientists said, I started to question it. I was already used to questioning what I learnt as part of my degree in electronics and computer and control engineering, but I tended to trust common scientific theories about life and its origins. It is surprising how easy it is to be relatively deep in our thoughts within a specific subject area, but very superficial outside of that subject.

We really need to take a step back and look at the bigger picture. I started to develop a greater trust for rational thoughts and question scientific theories. This distinction is so important and so obvious once it has been pointed out that it is surprising that so few of us make it.

The European church's historical suppression of science and reason has had a deep impact on the way we in Britain think today. It has become so much a part of our culture and is reinforced by constant references to the Dark ages, the Middle Ages with its church oppression and then the 'enlightenment' and 'scientific revolution'. School history seems almost entirely geared towards establishing a hatred of the past, a fear of dogma and religions in general and an enthusiasm for all things modern, scientific and secular. It is not that I now distrust all scientists, but now I trust my mind absolutely and them cautiously, with a pinch of salt. I'm now clear about the role of the mind and its limitations.

Philosophies

At school I had a few friends who would try to debate philosophical ideas. Some said that "we don't really exist" or "maybe we are just the figment of another creature's imagination" or "maybe another universe exists where all our rules of nature don't exist and, for example, people never die". The British have always been wary of such philosophical musings unlike other parts of Europe where it is considered an essential discipline to be able to think, like this, without limits. Therefore, I wasn't particularly affected by these thoughts, but if I did ponder upon them I became confused and unsure how to answer.

Through understanding the role of the mind such philosophical theories can easily be rejected as they have no basis in reality. The mind is incapable of producing a thought not based upon sensory input, or the memory of it, which is then linked to previous information. No one can imagine what infinity looks like, for example; hence we call it an imaginary number, as it has no place in our reality. Our reality is what we can sense, so philosophy, by definition is unreal. Such philosophies serve no useful purpose, as they do not help us to understand our reality further; rather they sometimes even contradict it. They should be written off as the frivolous games that they are.

It is not a philosophy to believe that Allah exists, even though we cannot describe Him in detail and have no sensory information about Him. It is a rational observation of our reality that leads to this rational conclusion. If we were to try to describe Allah further, then this would be philosophy as we have no sensory input about His essence. This is why Muslims are required to limit their thinking to the mind's limits and not assign the mind a role that it is unsuitable for. Once we confirm the basis of the revelation using our mind, then we accept all that is contained within it about Allah and the things that we have no sensory information about. These are outside of the mind's scope of judgment. So we believe in Allah, in His descriptions and names, in His books and messengers, in His angels, in the Day of Judgment, in heaven and hell and all else that is confirmed to be revelation.

In the Spectator magazine 8/11/2003 Nicolas Fearn writes on Alzheimer's: "The condition as good as demonstrates that there is no after life, because if you can be dead when you are alive, then you can certainly be dead when you are dead". This is an irrational conclusion, as it is an attempt to judge upon something that the author has no information about, neither sensory nor otherwise.

When Allah describes an aspect of the unseen for us then we accept it with all that the language it was described in implies. We don't then try to add to it or restrict it with our own minds. So, when Allah describes His mercy we accept it and believe in it, but we cannot quantify it with human mercy, as that is created and Allah's mercy is uncreated. We just stick to what the text said about it. Any further theorizing or philosophizing cannot benefit us due to its weak basis: the limited mind.

Is European Culture Universal?

Breaking out of the secular moulded way of thinking was not too difficult with some gentle guidance. One of the most important initial steps is to wake up to the fact that European thought is just that: European. It isn't a set of universal values that we just happen to have discovered. George Bush claimed in the build up to the spring 2003 Iraq invasion that "Freedom and democracy are not Western values, but are universal values for all people." This is false; rather, such values are a direct product of the unique European historical experience. Without the oppression of the church, its suppression of all scientific or rational enquiry or any idea that contradicted its dogma, and without the churches legitimization of the King's position, then the desire for reform, the resulting reaction to embrace all freedoms and the great resentment of religion would never have occurred. This lead to a final compromise solution that defies all ration and reason. It is solely a reaction to the European situation; far from universal.

Secularism was born and has been adopted as a solution to these historical problems. Either God does exist and therefore should have sovereignty over His creation, or He does not exist and so He has no sovereignty to give. But, to say that whether He exists or not doesn't matter and that the sovereignty in life's affairs belongs to the people and not God whose only domain is spiritual affairs, this is an irrational compromise between to opposites. How can two opposites be compromised with a third solution? Either a light is on or it is off, it cannot be somewhere in between. Compromise between two opposites is an irrational concept that contradicts reality and so the mind cannot accept it. It is upon a compromise that British secular culture is built. It is certainly not universal, rather a last desperate resort for weary Europeans tired of the fighting and conflicts. *Who could blame them for seeking a practical solution to end the conflict, yet it is time now for us to move on; its benefits were temporary and unsuitable for mankind to use as a basis for life. It is filled with contradictions and brings a whole host of new problems and oppression to replace that of the church and king. We now have the "democratic" tyrant instead of the autocratic king.*

A recent illustration of this came in a letter from a William MacMonagle of North Carolina when he wrote to the International Herald and Tribune (16/01/2004): "I have long admired the French approach to religion in public life. If the US had been through roughly 250 years of unabated religious warfare, it too would demand that religion remain a private affair. The only real hope for religious tolerance is to keep it off public display. Contrary to modern myth, religion is not the harmonizing influence its practitioners would have us believe. It is deeply divisive, and the drive to power in the name of anybody's god is the surest way for any country to come to grief. Religious practice should be held as a private matter, and it is in everyone's interest to keep it that way".

This serves as an illustration of the way that the European Christian experience has deeply affected our culture. It is worth noting here that the original American immigrants were in fact Europeans escaping from the same oppression.

It is common for us to regard all religions as the cause of disharmony and war, which is an extreme generalization. Not only did Islam not have a similar experience to the European Christians, so the analogy is false, but also this generalization disregards the real causes and circumstances of historical wars. Territorial claims have had a large part to play in the build up to many conflicts, recent as well as ancient. America's ideological dispute with the communist bloc was an ideological dispute. It was in the same class as the religious disputes that they so despise; one belief verses another. The two world wars had more to do with jealousy over the colonial spoils and checking the rising power of rival European states than any other factor; i.e. the balancing of powers.

It is nonsensical to consider that by removing spiritual beliefs from life, the cause of disputes will be removed too. This is a massive over simplification and a dangerous generalization.

It is wrong to compare Islamic history to the European Christian experience as they are very different in nature. Some publications often try to interpret Islam according to their own secular values, so everything nearing the author's own notions of freedom or gender equality (read sameness) is called enlightenment. It is simply just assumed that our secular British culture is correct (even though they vociferously deny any such notion of right and wrong). They try to use the terminology of European Christian schisms, to discredit Islam with. So we hear such terms as extremist, fundamentalist, militant, puritan, orthodox etc. banded around to draw contrast with the moderate and modern Muslims. All of these words are alien and meaningless when describing Islam. If an idea or rule is based upon an Islamic text then it is called Islamic, if not then it is called un-Islamic. There is no compromise or in between category, as to do so would necessarily be un-Islamic. If a person makes a sincere effort to understand a text and founds an opinion upon his understanding, then it is called an Islamic opinion, with the proviso being that the text supports the possibility of such an understanding. If his opinion was weak and he became convinced of a stronger interpretation then he leaves the older weaker one in favour of the newer stronger one. The Islamic texts are all in the Arabic language so his exertion of effort should be in that language in order to understand the text. If he became influenced by sources other than the texts, such as the majority view, or pressure from a foreign power, then his opinion is no longer an interpretation of the text, but derived from that other source, so it is no longer Islamic. Allah knows what is in the hearts of man so He will judge who is sincere in their adoption of ideas and who is not. In this life, we tolerate the different opinions as long as they do not contradict what is well established and impossible to have two opinions about, such as the obligation for a Muslim to pay *zakah* (annual wealth tax), pray five times daily or the prohibition of interest, adultery etc. However, when a person lives far away from the Islamic community and has no access to knowledge then his erroneous interpretation is forgiven as his ignorance is excused, until he knows better.

Many writers make no attempt to understand Islam, but just sneer at how backward Muslims are and how necessary it is for us to progress – i.e. become like them: reactionary, close minded and shallow. They assume that their own culture is so advanced and correct, when in fact the opposite is true. If the only point of reference is fourteenth century Europe, then it may well be an improvement; but if we compare our current situation to Islam, we can quickly see how backward it really is.

Freedoms

Upon this secular basis are built the freedoms we so adore in Britain. On them are built the so called "Human Rights". Then it is claimed that all this is basic for the human existence. Whilst it is true that European history is filled with repression, it is not correct to take the opposite knee-jerk reaction as a solution. The church forbade all speech that disagreed with its dogma, so we claimed that a basic "human right" is to be able to speak without any restriction; i.e. just the opposite reaction. The truth is that some things are false and should not be said, or permitted to be said, while others are true and should be said. Freedom of speech is in fact a fallacy. The examples of Western governments controlling what is allowed to be said and persecuting those who say what they don't want to be said requires a whole volume to catalogue. It is a part of daily life, and no one really believes they can say absolutely anything they want without prosecution (*or persecution*). Try calling for political Islam and you will soon find many barriers erected in your way. The communists found all of the same problems when they tried to propagate their views in 1950s America. The McCarthy hearings are infamous as an example of restricting free speech and opinion.

Freedom of speech never did exist and it never will. Restrictions will always have to be imposed. *The question is "who is to do the imposing, and according to what criteria?" As Muslims, we elect a leader to implement the restrictions laid down in the Qur'an and the teachings of the Prophet (May the blessings and peace of Allah be upon him).*

Reputation and honour are well understood, as today in Britain a man cannot be slandered, nor can a company be libelled without a case being taken to court to seek recompense for the consequences of such an attack. For a Muslim, his mother is an honour to be protected, so is his wife, but more than all other people, the Prophets are their most beloved, and of course honoured. Just as a company's image is of great value and is actively protected, so is that of Allah, the Prophets (peace be upon him all of them) and the message of Islam which is the legal foundation of an Islamic society.

My own imprisonment in Egypt was for propagating the ideas of Hizb ut-Tahrir. When a journalist asked one of our wives "is it not a contradiction that you criticise freedom of speech, yet you also criticise the imprisonment of your husband?" She replied "I am not calling for free speech in Egypt nor am I complaining about the lack of free speech in Egypt, rather I am complaining that my husband was imprisoned for speaking the truth about a dictatorial oppressive regime, which is something that all people should say." Hence, for us, freedom of speech is not a principle; rather upholding the truth is a principle; so the debate should be about "what things should be said and what should not?", rather than calling for the removal of all restrictions, which is impractical.

There is no Truth?

Equally fallacious is the rejection of truth through claiming that there is no truth, only differing opinions. Just because the past has shown conflicts based upon differences of opinion and the inability of the Europeans to discover the truth does not mean that the truth does not exist. This is just another knee-jerk reaction.

Islam is a truth with a proof and it is just simply wrong to claim otherwise. The solutions of the various Western philosophers to life's problems were often mistaken, just as the Roman culture, the Greek culture and the ancient Egyptian culture before it were also mistaken. Today we have simply found a more tolerable way of living with each other than our ancestors. Our modern way partially satisfies most of the people, but this does not make it correct. The basic beliefs in secularism and freedom have remained fairly constant since "the enlightenment', however the laws that make these principles exist in life have undergone constant tinkering and even replacement. What was once a moral value is now seen as abominable. Racism was once evidence of a good man, now it is outlawed. Multiculturalism was until recently the way for us all to live together, now it is seen as the cause of disenfranchisement of the community. Yet, after all of this changing happiness is still an unattainable goal for so many with only temporary contentment achievable.

We British have recently stumbled upon some semblances of decent human living, which Muslims knew for centuries. Then we claim that we invented it. For example, the right of the people to choose a ruler, representative government, the rule of law, women's rights including political participation and voting rights, protection of property, life, honour etc. We then mix these values up with other lesser values creating a contradictory mess, which we then call the most advanced and best civilization known to man. We'll all change our minds pretty soon, talk of the past as backward and claim that we have now discovered a new enlightenment and so are now the most advanced; the most right. How convenient to always be right, even though what we utter contradicts what we said yesterday.

When the real link is acknowledged between the multitude of worries and woes existent in our British daily life and the belief and values upon which culture and society are built, then the secular way of life does not seem so attractive after all.

Secular culture pretends that there is no right and no wrong as a principle in order to avoid disputes; then contradictions appear when some things are defined as right and others to be wrong. Twenty years ago I remember that open homosexuality was something that attracted a great deal of criticism and dislike. The worst insult in the playground was to be called "gay". Now it is the opposite; to criticise homosexuality is itself deserving of criticism. This is based upon the doctrine of tolerance which is considered to be ultimately "right" – but why? We answer: "because intolerance is just wrong!" Yet who will tolerate opposition to this principle? Or even tolerate criticism of homosexuality now? Islam clearly does not approve of homosexuality, so some won't tolerate Islam. Basically, we won't tolerate intolerance, so you have to conform to be tolerated. Assimilate in order to be accepted. We are so confused; filled with contradictions whenever something clashes with our interests or the latest fad.

The Islamic Vision

What person would knowingly want to live in a way that is contradictory and wrong? I didn't and I was concerned about the consequences of doing so. I decided that I wanted what was best in this life and in the next. I learned that Allah is a merciful Creator who sent many Messengers to mankind, and that final one He sent with a complete way of life for us to live by. Through reading how Islam solves human problems and how it averts the many difficulties that the secular culture has created in its wake, I was able to compare the misery guaranteed by continuing to live an un-Islamic life with the contentment assured from living an Islamic way of life.

Because Islam addresses the individual and his relationship with Allah, his relationship with himself and it also addresses the relationships in the whole society, then it is a complete alternative to the secular way of life.

Islam enjoins upon its followers the establishment of a state governed by Islamic rules. It has a unique political system with a fixed source for the rules by which the ruler and the people are held to account by the people. Its economic system clearly differentiates between public, private and state owned property. The people's basic necessities are protected whilst luxury items are traded freely, thus generating a thriving competitive private economy that is unable to usurp the essentials of people's lives. Hence, poverty is dealt with and opportunities for betterment and growth abound. All of this existed 1400 years ago and is still applicable today.

The difference between theory and practice does not exist with Islam, as it does with Capitalist economics. John Maynard Keynes is quoted as saying in 1933: "I was brought up, like most Englishmen, to respect free trade, not only as an economic doctrine which a rational and instructed person could not doubt, but also as a moral law", Yet the big headline American anti-trust cases, competition law and protectionist practices are the norm in Western countries. It makes you ask, just how free is free-trade? This contradiction was even highlighted by Adam Smith, one of the fathers of Capitalist economics, as can be seen from two of his well known quotes: "It is not from the benevolence of the butcher, the brewer or the baker that we expect our dinner, but from their regard to their own interest" which supports the laissez-faire approach of allowing competition to regulate the market place. He is also quoted as saying: "people of the same trade seldom meet together, even for merriment or diversion, but the conversation ends in conspiracy to raise prices." This second quote recognises that a completely 'free' market will not be in the public interest.

Islam does not suffer such contradictions as we do not claim the market to be free. We recognise the 'hands-off' approach of allowing market forces to determine the price according to supply and demand, but at the same time we are forbidden from engineering exploitative practices such as creating a monopolistic situation. Hence Islam contains mutually complementary rules, which people in Britain have just started to discover, as part of one complete economic system whose theory is the same as its practice. All of this existed fourteen hundred years ago.

As part of the social system that the Islamic State implements the roles of men and women are clearly defined. We do not pretend equality or consider men and women to be the same, as is the theory in the West. Rather, we recognise our natural differences and build the society according to what is suitable for each. Islam gave the women rights, security and dignity which secular societies still do not offer. A women in a secular society is often just a commodity; a piece of meat, whose value is measured in terms of her attractiveness. She is not safe to walk the streets, nor even in her own home, as she can easily become a victim of the ever increasing violent crimes or domestic violence. Islam gave women rights *to dignity*, to education, to vote, to earn and own money, to employ and be employed more than fourteen centuries ago. Again, all of this secular society has only just discovered, and some, such as honour, dignity and security, they still have yet to discover.

The Islamic state that we are calling for is a secure, peaceful state where the causes of crime are minimised and transgression dealt with harshly. At the same time it is a just state, where all people are equal before the law, regardless of race, gender or religion, and where miscarriages of justice are virtually unknown. It is a strong state that can deal with its enemies and protect its citizens. All of its population are citizens regardless of religion, gender or race. For the Muslims, spiritual contentment is achieved as they worship according to the Islamic way, assured in the promise of Allah's pleasure and reward in the next life. Non-Muslims are left to worship according to their own religions if they have one, and judged according to their own religion's laws in private matters concerning marriage, food, drink etc. It would be a truly ignorant or devious person who denied the tolerance afforded non-Muslim citizens of the Islamic state, both in the texts and in practice throughout history. If it was the plan of Muslims to annihilate all non-Muslims, then why are there still so many Christians, Jews, Hindus, Sikhs, Buddhists and others in the lands where Islam was dominant for centuries?

Mark Steyn wrote in the Spectator on 8th November 2003 "The Islamist goal is a planet on which their enemies are either dead or Muslim converts". Islam absolutely forbids the forcing of a non-Muslim to become a Muslim. Allah says clearly in the Qur'an **"There is no compulsion in religion"**.

Muslims seek to implement the Islamic systems in their lands without foreign colonialist interference. This just state will actively invite others to embrace Islam or to live as non-Muslim citizens, from where it is hoped that they will learn the truth about Islam, not the distorted lies that they used to hear, and so they too embrace Islam. However, they are free to choose and are not to be forced.

Look What I Discovered!

All this is what I learned about Islam in those first few weeks. I was amazed; amazed that all of this had been hidden from my view. Why was this not taught to every child at school, in a society that considers itself to be well informed? If I had not been willing to question my assumptions about my secular culture, it would all still be hidden from me. I thank Allah that He opened my heart to this.

I enthusiastically went to meet with some of my friends and family to tell them what I had discovered. I tried to relay all that I could, but I know I was poor at articulating it. I tried to focus on the proof of Allah's existence, proof of the Qur'an's authenticity, and the contrast between our secular values and that of Islam. Due to my lack of experience, I'm sure that I didn't do justice to the subject. I suspect that I just looked like a zealot who has found a new craze. All were generally polite, but at the same time, not really willing to be drawn into a debate about their own ideas. I understand this, as our British manner doesn't exactly encourage debate about religion and politics. In fact we loathe debating these two subjects more than any other. I myself had been through a long, slow process of discovering problems, considering solutions and then finding contradictions. This had continued until I discovered Islam, by which time I was willing to question my values and recognise Islam for what it is, the truth.

The main driving force for me was that I knew there was a problem and I wanted a solution, but it had to be the right solution. If one has not really concerned themselves to search for a solution, let alone the right one, then invitations to Islam must appear decidedly irrelevant. It really comes down to each person to think for them self.

One close friend responded "what about evolution?" So I said "what about it?" "It's been proven" he replied. "Who proved it?" I asked. "The scientists" he replied. He thought I was mad and said so, but I told him that my mind was made up. He rarely contacted me again, other than to say how disappointed he was or for occasional pleasantries. It just shows how weak our friendship had really been. We had shared a student house in the second year with two female students. We both enjoyed joking and partying together at the weekends. After I had chosen not to drink or go to bars anymore, it meant that we had little in common. The final straw for him was when I stopped visiting the house on account of not wanting to socialise with the girl who lived there. It wasn't that I disliked her, but Islam places tight restrictions on the relationship between men and women, and socializing in a private house is not permitted. Although we had lived in the same house for the previous year, we weren't especially close friends, she'd do her thing and I'd do mine. Occasionally we'd meet in the middle and go partying as a group. Once you remove the alcoholic socializing out of a relationship you'll be surprised how little is left.

A similar breakdown happened in my relationships with most of my other friends at the time, but not all. I try to keep contact with a few of them from my old home town, but we've drifted a lot. Living a large distance apart is certainly a factor; however, I do feel that my new beliefs have caused uneasiness. Few are prepared to talk about it. All in all, we have less in common to maintain the friendship. It's not difficult to remain polite acquaintances but that isn't the same as a real friendship. I have since come to develop some very close friendships with others.

Submission or Choice

One person close to me responded to my initial explanations of Islam with the comment: "I've got a new job, a new house, a new car and a new relationship. I'm happy and I don't want anything to change, so don't tell me anymore about your religion in case I feel that I have to change too". It showed me a great fear of change. It didn't occur to this person that becoming a Muslim doesn't imply rejecting a materially comfortable life or living a monastic life. This is an incorrect analogy between Christian philosophies and all other "religions". Islam is not an ascetic religion and there is no proof for the notion that we are composed of conflicting material and spiritual sides, so I don't accept it. On the contrary, Muslims are ordered not to reject their portion of this life and to seek the good of the life of this world as well as the good of the next life. Hence, the spiritual life, according to Islam, is to live our life in this world in accordance with Allah's rules for us, constantly aware of our relationship with Allah.

Despite the aspirations of many, nobody can live truly free, without limits. People always end up imposing limits upon themselves and their societies impose limits upon them. It is strange, though, to see how many of us in Britain despise for another to impose a limit upon us, even though it may be in our interest. Sometimes it is exactly the same way that we would choose to limit ourselves, given the choice. We reject the imposition as a matter of principle, even though nearly all of the rules in our society were not chosen by us but imposed without choice. It is just another glaring contradiction. The all important factor is choice, or at least the illusion of choice. I used to delude myself that I could exercise choice at any time if I so desired, yet practically it is not possible for me to do so. So, in reality, the sacred British value of freedom is just an illusion. It is all about feeling free, regardless of whether we are or not.

Muslims don't pretend to be completely free, having choice in all matters. We submit willingly to the limits and laws of Allah, not because we see the benefits in each one, but rather because they are Allah's limits, just that. That is our voluntary enslavement, our worship. Within the laws that Allah has legislated for us some actions are obligated, in which we have no choice and we do as much of them as we can. Others are an absolutely prohibited, except for compulsion or necessity. After that some things are recommended to do or to avoid, but we have the final choice in following the advice or not. In the final category we have been given free choice to do or not to do. These are the five categories of action contained in the Islamic texts.

A Muslim's attitude towards these rules, on a personal level, can be to follow them out of fear. He may do the bare minimum in this state, yet he hopes to be safe on the Day of Judgment. He could also yearn for the rewards of the next life, in which case he will follow more of the recommendations, so becoming a more complete believer. On top of this he could feel love for Allah so great and be filled with such gratitude that he starts to love all of what Allah loves and dislike all that He dislikes. The laws then become a moral guide for him, a guiding rope; information about his Lord's pleasure, rather than rope to tie him down.

On a societal level, these rules are moral values for the society to uphold, but they are also rigid rules to be obeyed. Just as any modern society has rules whose transgression is not tolerated, so it is with the Islamic society. It is not a matter of belief anymore, but a condition of citizenship that all obey the rules that make up the systems of the society and allow it to function.

I don't feel that Allah's limits oppress me at all. I have no natural instinct which must be suppressed as a result of being a Muslim. All of my natural desires are channelled and fulfilled in a way that Allah is pleased with, and I am pleased with. *I have been a captive in Egypt and then been released, so I can feel the difference between the two states. I realise that my feeling of freedom is relative not absolute.* I choose whether to obey Allah or not, yet I invariably choose what Islam prescribes as that is what I love, because that is what Allah loves. The limits to my daily life are fairly broad, so I am free to choose in most of my affairs, therefore I do feel free as a Muslim, relatively not absolutely.

The British fear of losing our choice leads many to object to Islam's imposing ways, while contradicting themselves. We are happy to accept the severe restrictions on alcohol and drugs but we oppose Islamic laws that do the same. *We now even have alcohol free zones in many town centres in the UK.* The net result is almost the same, as a non-Muslim in the Islamic state is not prevented from brewing his own beverages and consuming them in private, but he is forbidden to sell it or drinking it publicly among the Muslims. Many people have no desire to do this anyway, so why hate Islamic laws?

Most of us cover our bodies in the name of public decency and to hide our private parts, but we dislike the Islamic laws which do the same.

I feel that what causes opposition is the idea that "we might want to change the law at some point". This conflicts with the unchanging nature of Islam. Yet, how many of us honestly have a desire to encourage public nudity or open drunkenness? Those who do call for that often do so as a point of principle based upon upholding freedom, even if they don't wish to do the action itself. It is our hopeless love for freedom that causes such confusion, contradictions and problems. It will surely be our downfall if groups of liberal ideologues push the limits of acceptability further and further until our whole society implodes in lawlessness and anarchy.

We who live in a democracy today didn't actually choose most of the laws nor any the constitution; rather they were imposed upon us since birth and we are expected to conform. Nobody consulted us. Yet, most of us accept to have laws imposed upon us, even ones that we disagree with, as we understand the benefits, in terms of stability, that general conformity bring to our society. Frankly, an Islamic society would bring the same stability and many other advantages to the citizens' lives; whether that be in terms of comfort, family life, safety, justice, economic progress, education or political accountability. So, it is contradictory to oppose Islam because of its restrictions on choice, when we already have so little of it. We would do well to ponder on these contradictions and re-evaluate what we carry in terms of values and their basis.

Christian Belief and Contentment

Stuart, my Christian colleague at the cinema used to debate with me about our respective beliefs. I don't feel that it was correct, though, to use the word conviction for most of the Christians that I have come across. Since becoming a Muslim I have had discussions with Christians of all types: born-again Evangelical, Anglican, Catholic, Methodist, Jehovah's Witness, Seventh day Adventist, Orthodox etc. I have found that it is rare to meet anyone who has put any serious thinking into their belief. I've even been warned not to think, as "it will only lead you astray"!!! I was advised to just "follow your feelings" on so many occasions. It appears to me that, for a Christian, the feeling of contentment that one gets from believing Jesus is a saviour is the only proof that they have. Conversations always come back to this point.

I discussed with my mother's priest, who is a family friend, about the existence of God and the basis of our belief in Him. He commented that he had come across such an intellectual argument as the one I presented while he was studying at theological college. We agreed up to this point, but then the gap appeared as I continued to insist on building upon the same rational basis to prove the messenger's authenticity, whereas he preferred to follow his feelings to conclude that Christianity was correct. The basic point is that he could feel Jesus in his life, and this was all the proof he needed.

On another occasion I was at Speaker's Corner in Hyde Park London when I was confronted by a very rude preacher who tried to tell me that Muslims actually worship the moon. When that lie failed to move me, she asked me "why do Muslims only pray in Arabic? Can God only speak Arabic?" I said that we both worship the same creator. She said "no, you worship Allah and I worship God. They are two very different gods." An Egyptian Christian stepped in at that point to tell her that she is ignorant as he is a Christian Arab so calls his God by Allah, as it is His name in Arabic.

Another time I met a preacher outside Leyton station, started a conversation, then continued our debate into the evening on the phone. He said that what proved Christianity for him was that it answered the question of original sinfulness adequately for him. It didn't seem to occur to him that this is a Christian belief that, by definition, will have to be satisfied by Christianity. In my opinion, it is built upon a false premise. What can it mean to be born sinful? How can anyone know about sin if we are not told by our Creator what is right and wrong? Sinfulness isn't something that we can sense, naturally occurring. In reality we find that a person has the capacity to do either good or bad, according to his chosen morality. He can make mistakes or be weak as well as strong. So it comes down to "what is good and what is bad?" Neither good nor bad can be discovered by sense alone, as it is a quality that is assigned to actions and is external to them and not a part of them. Good for one person can be bad for another, if people are left to define good and bad according to their own desires.

We should, instead, rely upon news from our creator about what is good and bad, transmitted to us through revelation. We need to authenticate the source of the revelation before we can believe it to be correct, so it needs to have an independent proof. It is nonsense, therefore, to say that knowledge of sinfulness (which is only known after receiving revelation) is a proof for the correctness of the revelation.

I've not come across any more intellectual Christian proof than this, and even then it does not appear to be the basis for most Christians. The all important feeling is usually the real reason why the Christian remains a Christian, as even when I pointed out the inconsistencies or lack of reasoning, he'll defend his belief by mentioning the feeling.

In my experience in the UK it is only the Muslims who are actually challenging others to debate and use intellect as a basis of belief. Secularist and also the socialists share in that they both use a kind of deception to win debates. Secularists particularly love to bring up irrelevant comments about oppression by religion to win the debate and encourage a compromise solution. *Whether or not some religions did oppress people does not provide an evidence for the incorrectness of the belief, only that some people used it as a means to pacify and oppress others. Just as America and Britain today promote the slogans of democracy and human rights in the third world, but at the same time materially support the dictatorships that continually oppress their people. The incorrectness of these slogans is not established due to their abuse by some, rather it is their intellectual foundation that needs to be debated.*

Other religious people generally recognise that their belief is not based upon rational arguments. A Christian normally talks of his faith as oppose to his conviction or belief. Muslims, of course, have faith which is built upon trust, but it is a trust built upon a solid foundation which is a rational conviction. The English word faith is closer in meaning to the Arabic word "*tawakkul*" when Muslims use it, because it means that we trust in the help of Allah constantly. Our belief is not like a Christian's faith. Faith, as a basis for belief, implies a blind jump, without proof, so it is often referred to as a "leap of faith". Muslims use an Arabic word "*Iman*" to refer to their belief. It must be founded upon solid rational proofs, so there is no blind jumping. We don't say "we have faith that Allah exists", or that "we trust that Allah exists", rather we say that "we have *Iman* in Allah's existence", because we have no doubt whatsoever due to it being a rationally proven fact. Trust is then built upon that basis. Common English does not have an adequate word for translating *Iman*, but it could be described as a rational conviction, or a decisive ascent based upon rational proof. This is the meaning of *Iman* for Muslims, *even though sometimes we borrow the word faith, as it is just easier in conversation.* This is not mere semantics as there is a real difference between the two words' meanings.

The contented feeling that Christians claim comes about by having Jesus in their lives is not an exclusive feeling unique to Christians. It is quite normal for any person who believes in his religion to talk of such a feeling.

Do not all practitioners of other religions also get a feeling? Even those who worship idols do, because they feel that their prayers to them are being answered. I certainly feel that Allah has guided me and continues to guide me to the straight path. I feel that Allah is answering my prayers too.

All people have a spiritual instinct which drives us to recognise our weak nature and so revere what is greater, feeling humble in its presence. Due to this drive within us, we search for a god to worship. Some satisfy this drive through following a great leader, or a pop star. Others find stones or legendary gods to worship. Others discover the Creator who is much greater and more worthy of worship than all of His creation. Many religions have this in common. It is even said that the stone worshipping Arabs at the time of Muhammad (*May the blessings and peace of Allah be upon him*) believed in one creator, Allah Most high. The feeling of contentment then comes as a result of satisfying this instinct and is strengthened when we feel that we are on the true path and protected from evil. Anyone can feel it. Doubts, however, erode this feeling until it no longer provides any more satisfaction. If the basis of our faith is not rational, then the feeling will be temporary and it becomes necessary to block out all reason and to refuse to search for the doctrine's rational proof. Doubts remain, but are buried and ignored through constant distraction until they are forgotten.

As the Islamic belief does not contain any doubt, due to its rational basis that does not contradict with human nature, then the contentment that a Muslim feels is lasting and secure. Hence, Allah promised *"sakina"* (tranquillity) to the believers alone. They are those who believe that Jesus was a prophet and not the son of God and that Allah is one and not three.

My grandfather, after I had become a Muslim, complained to me that I "never really tried Christianity". When I was a teenager he would encourage me to be a more committed Christian, *but I wasn't really interested in religion at that stage*. I contended that it was not necessary to sample the feelings obtained from each religion to know which one is correct. It's not through trial and error, but through the mind that we recognise a fact from fiction. The mind is the arbiter of truth and falsehood, not how one feels. A person should allow his feelings to be shaped by his thoughts and never the other way around, as this would only lead him astray. Feelings are dangerous to follow as they are not consistent because they aren't founded on a firm basis. A person can feel good about something one day and bad about the same thing the next day. Rather, it is the mind that the feelings should follow; then they will be consistent.

Becoming a Muslim

I continued reading and discussing about Islam during the following weeks until on the second of December 1994 I said the *shahada* (testimony) in Arabic and English to formally acknowledge my acceptance of Islam as the truth and that I was now a Muslim.

After five weeks of contemplating, discussing, debate and reading, I had moved from a simple admiration to the aspects of the Islamic way of life, to a rational conviction in its beliefs and full acceptance that it, in its entirety, is the best way of life for me. At this point I was a believer in all but name, as I hadn't yet formally announced to anyone else my belief. A person is not considered in this life as a Muslim until he pronounces the *shahada* that "There is no god but Allah, and that Muhammad is his messenger".

I was travelling to a talk organised by the University of Westminster Islamic Society on my bicycle through London's Haymarket, where I had a near miss with a bus. I'd been a cyclist in London for a few years, so I'd had a number of near-misses and a few accidents, but this time I was more shaken up. It forced me to ponder "what if I died right now, how would I be judged; Muslim or non-Muslim?" I faced up to the fact that I believed in Islam and that this conviction wasn't going to go away. It was now up to me to proclaim this and live according to Islam with all of its rules. I mentioned my intention to my friend Asam at the talk. He grabbed the speaker who had given the talk, which I hadn't really been paying attention to; I had other things on my mind. We said the *shahada* "*Ash-hado allaa illaa ha illa-llaah, wa anna Muhammadar-Rasool-ullaah*" together piece by piece in Arabic. Then I repeated after him the English meaning of what I had just said "There is no god but Allah, and that Muhammad is his messenger".

At that moment I was formally a Muslim, *al-Hamdulillaah* (All Praise is for Allah). It was about 8pm on the second of December 1994.

In that hall there were about three hundred witnesses and about half of them came up to me to hug me and say "*As-Salaamu alaikum*", Peace be upon you, which is the Muslim's greeting for one another. It was quite an overwhelming reception. A small group of us went to Asam's flat in Camberwell that evening. Asam offered for me to sleep on his couch (he and his brother Qasim slept on the floor) for as long as I wanted. I did that for about four weeks to learn the basic Islamic rules and rituals of purity, prayer and so on. We continued our discussions every day to further develop and Islamic personality in me.

That first evening in the flat, Farhan was tough on me, telling me to have a shower, then to pray with them. Then he gave me a copy of the Qur'an as a present. He told me later that he had wanted me to realise how serious a commitment it is to become a Muslim and that my life had now changed. He hadn't wanted me to feel contented with just changing my belief without also changing my actions too. *Al-Hamdulillaah*, I wasn't about to do that. I have Allah to thank that he gave me such good people as friends when I most needed them.

Learning to pray wasn't difficult as I had already spent some time learning small pieces of the Qur'an mentioned in the Introduction to Islam book that I had bought a few weeks earlier. I had started praying sometimes in the evenings. Purification is also very natural to do, so it didn't take long to learn and get used to its details.

In reality, what changed the most from before were my concepts about how to live my life. My daily life did not undergo any immediate great upheaval, as I still went to work, still studied, still spent time with my friends and family, still exercised and still entertained myself. I had already stopped drinking and I had no girlfriend at the time, so nothing changed there.

News of my conversion to Islam spread around the university Muslim community. The next Friday I prayed the Friday prayer in the mosque in Goodge Street near to the university. Afterwards I found a group of colleagues from my course the previous year, who all came to greet me and say how pleased they were that I was now a Muslim. I was shocked. Here were fourteen Muslims in my class who had not even told me that they were Muslims, let alone try to explain their religion to me. On some occasions we would all be together in the student bar together. They may not have been drinking, but I had no suspicions that they might be Muslims. I had had so many questions about Islam; I would have loved to have had conversations with them. One closer friend had told me that he was an Arab, but it did not occur to me that he was a Muslim. He was as drunk as I was at weekends, so again it never occurred to me that he might be a Muslim.

I suspect now that the reason that they all kept it hidden from me was that Islam and Muslims generally had such a bad press, that they felt it better not to talk about their religion. British people are not exactly welcoming of religious discussions.

During the period immediately before declaring my Islam I had visited a mosque close to where I lived in South London. I was hungry for knowledge now, so I thought it natural to speak to Mosque Imam to enquire about introductory classes on Islam. I met him and the mosque committee drinking tea in the afternoon. I explained that I was very interested in finding out more about Islam. They left me standing in the door as they spoke amongst themselves, before telling me that they could only offer that I sit with the children learning to memorise the Arabic Qur'an; not exactly what I had in mind. As I left, I descended the stairs and met a younger Muslim coming up. He smiled and asked what I was doing there, so I explained. Again, I was shocked when all he did was smile again and say "good luck!"

Downstairs on the street was a small Islamic book shop, so I told the owner what had just happened. He felt bad for me, but his English wasn't great. He offered me a small book, then I went back on my way.

Again, I thank Allah that I already had met Muslims who were not afraid or lacking ability to explain Islam to.

Family Relationships

I went home to my parent's house that first Christmas holiday and spent time with them as normal. Christmas was always more of a family than a religious occasion in our home. Those who wanted to go to church would do so, then nothing more was mentioned about Christianity throughout the day. As I didn't go to church, the day was just a family gathering with food, games and gifts. Apart from when I was first married, or when I was overseas, I haven't missed our family gatherings.

My relationship with my immediate family has seen great improvement since I matured as a Muslim. I have always loved my family very much, but I wasn't very attentive to their needs while growing up as a teenager. I became distant and self-centred, and was basically a typical British adolescent. I've since come to learn just how abnormal such behaviour is for societies that still hold onto Islamic social values, such as Egypt, Turkey or Pakistan. It is almost unheard of for teenagers to take their frustrations out on their parents or to show any disrespect to them. However, for teenagers growing up in the UK it is considered normal to answer back and show ingratitude to parents, who patiently wait for them to "grow out of it." As a result, I shut myself away from my family, becoming distant as I spent most of my time outside of the house with my friends, or isolated in my room. I treated my parent's house more as a hotel than a home to be shared.

Islam places a great emphasis on the family relationship and the respect and gratitude that a Muslim must always show his parents, so I started to increase my efforts to stay close to mine. *Although I live a distance from my parents now,* I try to keep regular contact as much as I can. The biggest change is in my attitude. I now consider a close, warm relationship to be much more important that I did before.

Changed Personality

As I have mentioned before, one of the most important concepts that I now carry is about the role of the mind and its limits. If my belief is built upon the mind then it is not a doubtful matter and will be a solid foundation for my life, as long as I remember it and actually refer to it. It isn't enough to just have a belief, but that belief has to be explicitly linked to my other thoughts, emotions and actions in order to serve as a basis for me and be influential in my life.

We should know that some aspects of our life we do not control, whereas other aspects we are in control of. For example, a person could be very used to having relationships outside of marriage such that if he was told to stop, he'd find it very hard or maybe he'd even claim it is impossible. However, he should know that his desires are within his capability to control and that they should not be left to control him. If he forces himself to put his thoughts about it into perspective, then he can change his view about it and even no longer desire to do so anymore. He is in control of what to think about, so he can affect a change on his own. If he forces himself to ponder Allah's rule on the subject of casual relationships and girlfriends, then he will know that this is something that makes Allah angry, and that Allah has prepared a punishment for the one who succumbs to their desires having such relationships. He could further consider his gratitude that Allah has created him, then out of love for Him, preferring Allah's pleasure to his own, change his desire for casual relationships into a dislike for it. He'll look at women in a different way, with respect and not just as mere objects, as this is what Islam encourages. He'd still find them attractive, were he to ponder on it, but he tries to avoid such thoughts as they don't benefit him except in the context of marriage.

Thus he can control his emotions and desires through controlling his thoughts.

If he found himself in an environment where he was tempted, then he can remove himself from that place. If he regularly forgot to remember the hellfire while in such situations, then he can set reminders for himself, or ask others to remind him, or even train his mind to remember. This way, he remains in control. *He is not denying his desire, but he is channelling its satisfaction through a permissible way, hence feeling uplifted physically, emotionally and spiritually. Far from suppressing natural instincts and needs, Islam encourages their fulfilment; however, it does not leave the person to be a slave to his desires. What separates humans from animals is our ability to think and so choose when and how to satisfy our instincts. To be a slave to our whims is not befitting the peak of creation, mankind.*

Casual relationships were so normal for my circle of friends, but I was able to put a lid on it in exactly the way mentioned above.

Another example for Muslims is waking up to pray the Morning Prayer. Sometimes it can be difficult to get out of bed at four in the morning, which translates to desiring sleep more than prayer. If I remember that the hellfire is waiting for me if I don't pray, then preferring the prayer to sleep is easy. If I consider my love for Allah, and why He deserves to be loved over all else, then the desire to worship Him grows stronger and I feel ashamed to deny Him what he wants me to do. Again, I'm in control of changing my desires through thought. I can use any means to remind myself of whatever it is that provides me with motivation. Islam addresses this, so Muslims are encouraged to remember Allah at every action they perform. The call for prayer in the morning even includes the phrase "prayer is better than sleep", encouraging us to change desires in accordance with what Allah informs us of what is good and bad. For most daily actions, the Prophet (*May the blessings and peace of Allah be upon him*) taught us a prayer to say with it.

Still with the example of rising from bed, if I was finding difficulty in getting out of bed to go to work, then it only takes a simple thought about the adverse consequences of losing my job to provide enough motivation to do so. Moreover, if I was due a bonus for coming to work on time, then I'd enthusiastically get out of bed early when I remembered it. If I further remembered that my boss would be upset, and that this is a person whom I have great respect and gratitude for, then I would find the motivation to overcome the tiredness and happily go in to work. All of this is because the link between my desire and the action have become clear to me at that moment. So, the real issue is comparing my desire to the consequence and deciding which one I prefer.

I remember, years later, that I found it easy to get out of bed to comfort my son in the night, because my love for him was greater than my desire for sleep at that time. *Putting matters into perspective is crucial. The Prophet (May the blessings and peace of Allah be upon him) further helped us with this when he said "The two morning prostrations are better than the world and all that is in it."*

Why mention all of this fairly obvious stuff? Well, my point here is that we should not feel trapped into doing actions which Islam disapproves of, nor should we wait patiently to be changed by some external force. Rather, we should realise that we have the ability to change ourselves by putting things into the correct perspective; meaning: to clarify the link between our thoughts, emotions, actions and our belief.

No one should think that following Islam would be difficult with all of its rules. All of us in the world are living within a set of rules. If we evaluated their worthiness to be adhered to, based upon their origin, we'd quickly see that the rules of the Creator are far superior to those invented by people, thus we'd desire these superior rules above all others; regardless of what we currently want. Desires can be changed, so we can perfectly happily want only what Allah likes and dislike all that Allah dislikes. All this, as long as we can link each issue back to belief. When we do this we remain in control of our thoughts and desires, not allowing ourselves to be controlled by random desires and external stimuli.

Emotions such as happiness, fear, sadness etc. are naturally produced according to our concepts about how to satisfy our instincts. We have a choice to be controlled by them, or to control them. "Pulling one's self together" is something we've all had to do from time to time. How successful we are depends upon how in control of our thoughts, and hence, our emotions we are. Controlling emotions is about keeping them within acceptable limits, by channelling them and putting them into context through thought. This is neither suppressing them nor bottling them up.

Islam encourages contemplating to link all thoughts and emotions to the solid belief and made this linkage the basis of the Islamic personality. Simply believing in Islam as the truth does not mean that I have an Islamic personality. Not until I actually allow that belief to govern my every thought and, hence, influence my feelings and actions, can my personality be described as Islamic.

Sadly, the understanding of Islam amongst many Muslims was generally weak, so it was normal to meet Muslims whose personalities were not

Islamic. They may even display qualities which appear Islamic. Maybe they pray, fast Ramadan, avoid major sins or have pleasant manners, yet this alone is not enough to describe their personalities as Islamic, because these are actions and the personality is not comprised only of actions. The true distinguishing factor of any personality is the thought upon which it is based and the way that these thoughts affect and manifest themselves in actions. Thus, although a Muslim may have fine manners, it may be easy for this person to make compromises in economic, political or social matters, as he doesn't consider that Islam is concerned with them, other than in a generally moral way. He may speak about the spirit of Islam as an excuse for leaving the detailed rules, for example. His thoughts about daily life and his concepts about solving problems are driven by other than Islam; perhaps his desires, philosophies or trendy theories. As long as these can become a basis for some of his thoughts, then his personality is contradictory, confused and therefore not Islamic. No one should deny him his *Iman,* labelling him a non-believer, as this may not be the case; he is still a Muslim and a believer as long as he does not reject the Islamic belief (*Aqeedah*). However, the form of his personality is contrary to the form that Islam seeks to create in people, due to the impurity of his thought's reference point. Thus, he must get in contact with his own thoughts, constantly re-addressing them to ensure that they are solely built upon the Islamic texts and nothing else. Whenever he is presented with a new idea, he must refer to what Islam says on it before he attempts to give his own judgment on it. When this becomes his habit, then and only then, can his personality be described as Islamic. As an analogy, consider a judge who is a Muslim, but he judges in an English court according to the English law. Can this judge be called an Islamic judge, when Islam plays no part in his judgments? The subject of describing our thoughts is similar to this; it is all about how we make judgements; upon what basis? Islam or something else?

Fate and Fatalism

As I mentioned, in daily interactions with Muslims it was common to find un-Islamic personalities, ranging from those who resemble secular British people in almost every aspect, to those who outwardly appear very Islamic. Naturally, as a relatively new Muslim it was often assumed that I must have a very basic understanding of Islam, so I often got asked "Do you pray?" When I replied in the affirmative I would sometimes then get asked "all five daily prayers?!!" This reflected a common mentality among some Muslims; that prayer is something difficult to be constant with. It is felt that the feeling of having strength enough to pray is something not normal and very hard to obtain; even it is out of our control. If this were true, then why will we be accounted in the next life according as to whether we prayed or not? Why punish a people for neglecting a duty that they were powerless to perform?

Allah says "Allah does not charge a soul except according to its capability" so, if it is true that we really are not able to perform it, then we are excused. If, on the other hand, we are capable, but just making an excuse for ourselves, then we are still accountable. The point here is that we are capable of gathering the strength to pray as long as we remain in control of our thoughts, which is the normal state for most human beings. We are characterised by the fact that we are able to choose. Allah has shown us through revelation the two paths of right and wrong; it is up to us to choose which one to follow and we are accounted on the Day of Judgment according to how we made these choices.

It is wrong to consider the path to being able to pray as being long and difficult, as it is simply a matter of considering our belief at the time of considering the prayer, thereby acknowledging the link between them both and so developing a view towards prayer based upon this link. This requires an initial intellectual effort until it becomes a fixed concept. It is more difficult to preserve this link at all times as it may slip or be forgotten, so concerned Muslims make many extra prayers and read Allah's words regularly to ensure that they stay in a state of remembrance, remaining grateful and God fearing. Whilst forgetfulness and temptation remain out of our control, thinking and doing actions to encourage remembrance are firmly within our ability to control.

It is not correct to passively await change, as the initiative must begin within us. I often used to hear "I will pray when Allah wills me to pray" or "I will pray when I become strong enough". Saying this is attributing the responsibility to change to an external factor and not recognizing our own role, which is to use the ability to choose that Allah has given us. No one should make the mistake of limiting Allah's will to our own desires, as to do so is a grave error. Allah's knowledge is complete and so He knows what choices we will make, yet we still have to make them, as our knowledge is incomplete and we remain able to choose right from wrong and will be accounted accordingly. Allah's knowledge is a completely separate subject from our ability to choose. It is Allah's will that we are able to make choices.

'Umar bin al-Khattaab, one of the companions of the Prophet (*May the blessings and peace of Allah be upon him*) once asked a man who openly drank some wine why he did it. The man replied "it was Allah's will for me to drink it". He tried to excuse himself with his philosophy that he isn't responsible for his choices. To this 'Umar responded "then it is Allah's will that I punish you".

No one should passively await change, making excuses such as "I am not as strong as the Prophet's companions were". Rather, we should be aware of our own weakness and seek to change it through our thoughts and whatever series of actions may be necessary to assist in this. If we don't fear the fire, then we should read about it until we become aware of its description and how painful it would be. If we don't have enough love or gratitude for Allah, then we should contemplate on his mercy and love for us. If we don't understand a matter then we should seek its understanding from those who do. If the atmosphere around our friends and colleagues weaken us, then we should try changing that atmosphere, or leave them if they refuse to change. If we are forgetful, then we should devise plans to remind ourselves. We keep doing this until all of the obstacles have been removed that prevent us from being constant in our worship of Allah.

Solid belief demands that it be a basis for thoughts and so lead to desires and emotions being built upon it, and then leading to actions being built upon it too.

It is highly contradictory that a person remains passive in matters of Islamic rules, yet very active in matters related to worldly pleasures. If I am hungry, I take an action to prepare some food. If I want to get married then I look for a bride. I shouldn't passively await change from an external source. I shouldn't say "my hunger will go when Allah wills" doing nothing to feed myself. It is true that nothing happens without Allah's will, but that is a different subject to the actions we are required to do to initiate a change.

A man came to the Prophet (*May the blessings and peace of Allah be upon him*) complaining that his camel was lost. When the Prophet (*May the blessings and peace of Allah be upon him*) asked if he had tied it, the man replied "I had reliance (*tawakkul*) on Allah to protect it". The prophet (*May the blessings and peace of Allah be upon him*) told him to "Tie it AND have *tawakkul*". Thus, one is not dependant on the other, nor is one the substitute for the other. Rather, they are two separate subjects that go hand in hand together. The meaning is: do what you are able to do and trust in Allah, at the same time, in the matters that are out of your control.

We believe in fate and destiny but we are not fatalistic. We recognise the matters that we do control, so we concern ourselves with them, and we leave the matters that we don't control. There is no excuse for anyone to choose not to pray. Allah has commanded decisively for all mankind to believe in Him and to pray to Him, so we should all respond to His call, as much as we have the ability to do so.

Accessing Information about Islam

For all the talk of free speech and a free press in Britain, it is surprising how hard it is to find accurate information about Islam. It may be possible to actually publish a book or paper about Islam, but it is very hard to get it distributed, so it remains effectively hidden from mainstream view. Many of us in Britain consider ourselves to be well informed, believing the hype about what a free society we live in, as the free availability of information ensures that all viewpoints are represented. In the past ten years that I have been a Muslim, I have not once see Islam represented in the mainstream British television or newspaper media. Whenever Islam is discussed it invariably takes the form of an attack by someone calling for secularism, then maybe a rebuttal by a so-called "representative of the Muslim community" or a "community leader," who is only offering a moderate defence of Muslims and is in fact building his defence upon secular concepts. In short, he is never an Islamic personality. These so-called community leaders are always news to us Muslims, as we rarely know how they came to represent us when they are only representing secular politics. A true leader would have a large following, yet these media friendly appointed leaders usually have none.

Effectively, the average British person, who does not undertake a detailed search for the truth, will only hear two sides of the same secular coin. This is an effective control of opinions as it is expected that the majority of us will follow sheep-like, while feeling comforted at how "free" and "well-informed" we are; when in reality we never get to hear that there exists an alternative point of view. The standard of reporting and commentary on Islam and Muslims in Britain is very poor and can often appear overwhelmingly dishonest. Journalism generally seems to look down with pity on 'the other', assuming our own reference point to be unquestionably superior and correct. It favours tugging on our emotions, rather than debating ideas.

I remember when I was growing up the effect that this kind of loaded journalism had on my viewpoint towards Communist Russia. I remember the use of emotion and sensationalism whenever journalists reported on the differences between Russia and Britain. Communist Russia was portrayed as bad, while Gorbachev's "Perestroika" and "Glasnost" reforms were invariably reported as a good thing. Rarely, however, was the question asked "why are they good?" More honest journalism should have discussed the ideological differences between the two societies, as these are the real fundamental differences, which then lead to the country's economic circumstances. Instead they focused on how much healthier Britain's economy was. Dry intellectual discussions are not nearly as appealing as playing with people's emotions; through comments and images alluding to how "it's not right to have so little choice in the shops" and "why are the people having to endure such poverty?" The predominant image of Russia from the 1980s media was the long queues for food outside empty shops. Such tugging at our emotions ignores the fact that Britain's own colonialist policies enforce poverty on millions in the third world of Africa and Asia. Moreover, Capitalism's own economic principles don't recognise the right to a decent living for everyone, as wealth is considered to be a reward for those who are productive and not a basic right. It is a fundamental belief of Capitalist economics which views the "free market" as the principle means of distribution of wealth, so the cake gets shared according to the effort one puts in, in theory, but according to the power and influence one can yield, in practice. This inevitably leads to a state where some have plenty and others have little, maybe even perish. This is evident when one looks to the poverty existent in the US, UK and EU. How many poor people suffer from disease, hunger, cold or lack of medication each year? The welfare policies of these countries are only an 'Elastoplast' solution, which contradicts Capitalist ideological principles, but assist in quelling rebellion and dissent, hence are adopted on this basis alone. Such measures are tolerated, but not believed in, as being temporarily necessary measures, for as long as the possibility of mass rebellion remains. However, rightwing politicians are constantly trying to reduce public spending by privatising welfare institutions, such as healthcare and pensions, and so implement ever purer Capitalist policies.

None of this was mentioned in the popular media though. The Communist ideas were not publicly debated alongside the Capitalist ideas. Capitalism, with all its flaws was automatically assumed to be superior and dislike for Communism was developed on the basis of the economic misery that it led to. That was the diet of 'own-trumpet blowing' that my generation was subjected to through the TV and print media. The cause of the differences were not looked at, only the consequences. Evaluating the merits of the secular belief is not exactly at the heart of British journalism.

The effect of such emotional reporting and commentary rubs off on us ordinary folk, who start to consider ourselves enlightened, well informed and nobody's fool, yet we are actually being conned into supporting nonsense and contradictions. A quote from the Daily Telegraph of 15th January 2004 illustrates this point. Excerpts from Sgt. Steven Roberts' audio diary of 23rd March 2003 were printed, in which he was speaking from Iraq during the occupation: "I know why I am over here. Because children are walking around with bare feet, ill fitting and tatty old clothes and we are over here to free them from the regime so they can grow up to be and do what they want." However, it is obvious that Bush and Blair's war had nothing to do with solving Iraq's poverty, as it was the US and UK colonial policies that created it in the first place. The way that Sgt.

Roberts links his emotions at seeing the state of a third world economy for the first time to the righteousness of his own country's situation, is a reflection of how we are gripped by the dishonest reports in the media. We're all just so sure that our "good ol' freedom and democracy" at home can't be wrong.

Almost all third world countries have similar sights to be seen, barefoot and tatty children with little prospect for the future, even in some Western countries too. India, a democracy, has children dying in the streets from hunger on a daily basis. Britain and the US have thousands of malnourished children with ill-fitting, tatty clothes, worn out shoes, not having any chance to fulfil their dreams due to their poverty. No, the reason for the war on Iraq had nothing to do with alleviating the people from their poverty. It was not motivated by a humanitarian concern for less privileged people.

Moreover, simply ridding the Iraqis of Saddam will not enable them to pursue their dreams, unless they happen to dream of being colonial servants to the new American Capitalist empire, having no other aspiration than to slave away, enriching company directors and foreign shareholders (along with a few token Iraqis), hoping one day to retire with a few material possessions before they die, only to face their Lord and be accounted for neglecting the Islamic rules and replacing them with foreign Capitalist ones. This may well be the dream in the West, so it's understandable that we may rather superficially guess it to be the goal of every Iraqi. However, this dream is a derivative of the secular thought which makes expediency the highest value. But, most Iraqis are Muslims who have different beliefs, a different view on life, and therefore different values and dreams. Merely replacing one oppressive dictatorial regime with another, even if it is called a democracy, will not bring them any closer to realizing their dreams. We are allowing ourselves to be fooled by our own journalists if we think this to be the case.

While here in Egypt, during the 2003 Iraq war, I watched the TV footage from the Arab media and also read some of the British and American newspapers. It was as if they were reporting on two different wars. The Western journalists managed to find odd individuals describing the Iraqi joy at being "liberated" (occupied). Whereas the Arab media focused on showing how Iraqis were not relishing the idea of occupation ("liberation"). It's true that Saddam was hated, but that does not mean that Bush, his replacement, is loved.

This should not come as a surprise when we consider the contradictory nature of the most fundamental Western beliefs; such as secularism, freedom, pluralism and democracy. All of these so-called standards and principles that Britain and America are constantly calling for overseas are actually double standards, so easily contradicted when a benefit is perceived in doing so.

Faced with this kind of journalism, what chance does Islam have to occupy any space in the popular media?

Preventing the truth being heard extends beyond the mainstream media in Britain. Public talks get banned, room bookings are not approved, radio licenses get cancelled, Student Union societies get banned, active students get removed or expelled from universities on trumped up charges, posters are pulled down, newspaper adverts refused, Mosques ban discussion meetings, etc; along with a whole raft of other dirty tricks to ensure that any discussion of non-secular Islam is very small-scale and never hits the mainstream. All of this I have personally witnessed since becoming a Muslim actively involved with calling to Islam in Britain.

Those who do challenge the Capitalist values have to get through so many obstacles to get heard that generally they are never seen as a real threat, so are tolerated. If they start to make headway, then the defamation campaign starts and the whole media apparatus turns to ridicule the challenger, thus making sure that he poses no serious challenge. Serious debate will rarely ever be entertained. So, occasional demonstrations of anger or permitting limited dissenting voices to be heard is done more as a token gesture to give the illusion that free speech exists and to absorb people's frustrations.

At the time of writing this, France is in the process of banning school girls from wearing the Islamic headscarf, *al-Khimaar* or *Hijab*. Many media voices are angrily claiming that the *Hijab* is an expression of extremism, or that it is a symbol of male oppression over women etc. These are the people that claim to promise freedom to behave as one likes, or to worship as one likes, or to say what one likes. The condition is, however, that you just have to happen to want to say and do only what conforms to the secular culture. I'm amazed at how few people notice this contradiction, which exposes the whole secular freedom loving culture as an impractical fraud.

It is also surprising how few of us are willing to acknowledge the link between our over sexualizing the female image and the sexual harassment and misogyny which is so common today in Britain. It has reached the point that a woman is not free at all to choose what clothes to wear, even if she wants to cover her body and not be on display for all men to enjoy. She is under intense pressure to conform to the sexualised clothing standards as a display of her "freedom", "choice", "equality" and of course her "independence". Strangely, however, men are under no pressure to wear micro-mini shorts or to prove how equal they are to women. Just another hypocrisy to be expected from the secular culture. If we were to publicly acknowledge the dire consequences of too much freedom, then we may start to actually question just how valid a value is it?

The *Hijab* is outdoors clothing for Muslim women to wear as an act of obedience to Allah. It is not a man-made obligation and not an oppression, but truly it is a liberation from being viewed as merely an inferior object. It allows a woman to deal with men in society on secure and dignified terms as the sexual element to their interaction is reduced. Furthermore, in an Islamic society, the view towards women is that she is an honour to be protected and not exploited, so the *Hijab* elevates her status and is in keeping with the objectives of the society.

Ramon Rodriguez, a writer from California, wrote in the International Herald and Tribune on the 9th February 2004:

"Super Bowl XXXVIII is one or the history books, but for all the wrong reasons. What all of us witnessed a week ago was the very worst of America put on global display for all the world to see. The Janet Jackson-Justin Timberlake incident was only one of a series of excesses that built one upon another until Janet Jackson's bodice was ripped away by Timberlake, revealing a breast. Imagine how people in the Middle East are going to react to this display, with its implications of Western decadence and exploitation, at a time when we are urging them to follow the American example, especially with regard to women. Is nothing sacred? Is there anything that our children can enjoy or partake in that has not yet been adulterated? What has happened in the United States of America that has led the bosses of the National Football League and CBS to think they could get away with foisting such a disgusting exhibition of excess on Americans? For one, we exist in a palpable and tangible culture of sex and violence, with the misogynist strains of "modern youth music" proudly on display, with young males being taught to disrespect females, perhaps even to scorn them or hold them in contempt. The Super Bowl halftime fiasco represents a new low in American vulgarity and sexism."

A rare voice indeed!

Carrying the *Da'awa* / Studying Arabic

After I had become a Muslim, I started to spend time with the people who had helped me to discover Islam. We went to Cambridge every Saturday for a few months to establish a *da'awa* (invitation) stall in the main shopping street. It was basically a couple of pasting tables covered in free leaflet and some books. We also had large provocative posters on boards saying "Communism is dead, Capitalism is dying, Islam is alive" etc. Our objective was to meet with the ordinary people and the intellectual elite of Britain to discuss the matter of Islam. We did get a number of conversations from the local population and some students of the university.

During the summer of 1995 I spent most of my free time in the British library, either at the old Oriental and India office or the main reading room in Bloomsbury. I was slowly going through the entire Orientalist collection which discussed the early Islamic period of Muhammad's life and the four rightly guided caliphs (successors of the prophet in ruling). I was researching that period as it is the model period for Muslims. It is the time when Islam was implemented by rulers whose honesty was legendary; hence corruption was an absolute low.

I learned a lot about the differing views related to Islam as a political way of life, particularly as most of the authors, being Orientalists, started from the basis that Islam was inherently evil and needed to be exposed. Their approach was invariably to find fault, even if they had to twist the texts to get there. Some of the books that I read were written by Muslims whose sole sources of reference were other Orientalist books. Very few writers on Islam, who write in the English language, were able to access the many original Arabic books on Islam, so they relied on regurgitating what a few Orientalists have written years before. These are usually inaccurate and influenced by the time in which they were written. I found books that tried to prove the case for denying any political dimension to Islam; attributing all Islamic politics to the innovations of the first four caliphs. This was a common insinuation in the Orientalist books, but screams of ignorance, as one only has to open any book of *ahadeeth* (sayings of the Prophet (*May the blessings and peace of Allah be upon him*)) to see the tens of statements he made related to affairs of state. It comes as no surprise that many of these early Orientalist source books were written during the British Raj period, when Britain was colonising India and was actively trying to persuade the Muslims there to accept foreign rule and concentrate on spiritual matter.

In 1995 there were only a few books about Islam that had been translated from Arabic into English. These are generally more accurate due to being better researched, as the author has hundreds of years of writings on Islam at his fingertips, including the original sources.

I had concerns that I was taking so much of my religion based upon trust and imitation of those around me. I had not doubted in the importance of the work to bring Islam back to life, or the fact of its decline in the world today, but I wanted to be convinced of the evidences that the scholars used to extract their understandings or to be able to adjust my own understanding, if I saw weaknesses. I wanted the truth or as close to it as I could get. I wanted to feel emotionally connected to the rules that I obeyed in my life, not taking them by way of imitation; if the one I imitated changed then the rules I followed would change too. I wanted orthodox Islam that the Prophet (*May the blessings and peace of Allah be upon him*) had brought and that his companions had carried and taught, whom he was pleased with when he died.

Learning Arabic was the key to all of this, so I had a plan to do so as soon as I was able.

I started learning Arabic at my university as the final elective unit to obtain my engineering degree. During the second semester of this course, after I had graduated, I started a job fixing Sony Playstations which clashed with the lesson times, so I had to drop out. I later tried self study courses but to no avail. Time organisation was always the problem. Beginning learning a new language is an uphill struggle, so it is easy to lose motivation when the going gets tough. Not being in the environment where the language is used is also a major obstacle, as there is little opportunity to consolidate the new vocabulary and grammar learnt.

I resolved to study Arabic in an Arab country at the first opportunity. I knew that as you, my son, grew you will need stability in terms of schooling, so as you were only one years old, it was the best opportunity to travel abroad. As a family we planned for ourselves two or three years to learn the language well, then we'd be free to live wherever we chose.

Finished *Al-Hamdulillah* on 7th March 2004

This is then end of my explanation for my son. I sent many letters through the official channels, but this one I had to keep hidden whenever a prison inspection came. Finding hiding places was not easy, but I found that I could roll the pages and put them inside a pole used to hand the shower curtain. I had intended to continue with the events leading up to my arrest and imprisonment, but as the trial was still ongoing, I decided that it was too risky, so stopped writing at the point when I arrived in Egypt. I made notes about the prison life, but left the full write-up until I returned. I hoped when writing it that my son would read it when he grows up, so that he could know about me and why I chose the path that I did. I did not know whether I would ever see him again, or how much he would be a part of my life in the future. I was surrounded by prisoners who had finished their sentences long ago, or who had never seen a judge and who had lost all hope of knowing their children again.

Part 2

There are many stories that have been left untold, but what follows are the main events of my incarceration, as well as a few stories to give a glimpse of what prison life in Mubarak's Egypt was like. The people I met all have stories to tell, however many cannot yet be told as they are not yet out of the woods, with their future still very uncertain. In a few places I have changed names, as it may not be desirable or even safe for their true identity to be known.

Most of this text was written immediately after I returned to the UK, although a few additions were made more recently. As I type this introduction, I have just heard reports that Hosni Mubarak is critically unwell, after spending some time in the very prison that I was in. I had also heard that his two sons and much of his government were actually incarcerated in the same cells that I used to frequent, during my stay in Mazra'a Tora prison near Cairo.

Egypt

I first arrived in Egypt on the first of January 2001. I was met at the airport by a friend from England, Reza who was already living in Cairo. He had moved to be closer to his mother whose husband was an ex-pat engineering Consultant there. I hadn't known he was there until weeks before I was to travel. I stayed in a mutual friend's flat, who was away studying in America. I was to share that flat with Badr, who was a student at al-Azhar University in Cairo.

I chose Egypt because it is the home of al-Fagr centre for teaching Arabic to foreigners. The website was impressive, but when I arrived I found that the prices were more than those quoted online I realized that I had only enough savings to last just three months if I studied with them, so I decided to hire a cheaper private tutor to teach my wife and I.

After I had settled into our new accommodation, I met my wife and son at the airport and we started to adjust to life in Egypt. The pollution was shocking, the noise equally so, as was the treacherous traffic system, or lack thereof. We got used to it in time though and started to feel at home.

We found the Egyptians to be so friendly and welcoming. Our new neighbours invited us round for dinner and tea. The local businessmen gave us lots of help and were generally very generous with us. Those who work around the tourist sites and a lot of the taxi drivers saw us as a source of revenue, and were much more greedy than they were friendly. However, just by moving away from those areas by only a few streets we met genuine people who wanted only to be friendly and generous. I had a few arguments with taxi drivers over the hugely inflated fare, but always locals stepped in to assist me. Egyptians love to be helpful.

On the metro trains, my son was the centre of attention, as all Egyptians, young and old, men and women, absolutely love children. Complete strangers would entertain him for the whole journey. In the supermarket, sales assistants would stop their work to play football with him in the aisles. I was really enjoying living in Cairo.

After three months, my studies were not going according to plan. My tutor had relied heavily on teaching me the grammar rules of Arabic in English. I had a good understanding of very detailed rules, but lacked the vocabulary to use it. Another problem was that the average Egyptian speaks a colloquial dialect of Arabic, while I was learning the pure Arabic, which is well understood, but generally reserved for writing, speeches and broadcasts.

This meant that it was hard for me to practise what I was learning. The friends that I was making, generally spoke in English and were enjoying the chance to practise their language skills, but that didn't help me much to develop my own.

I had met an Egyptian man in a mosque just a few weeks before I left London. When he heard that I was soon travelling to Cairo, he gave me his number and invited me to visit. He turned out to be the mayor of his village and the surrounding municipality, as well as the local head teacher and English teacher. Again I didn't get much chance to practise Arabic with him. When we did visit his village, he introduced me to many people, but only the English students could I really form any friendship with. One lad, Shareef, became a good friend showing me around his village and Cairo, even though we only spoke in English.

In order to stay in Cairo, I needed to earn some more money, so I found a job as IT Manager of a small internet start-up company. The staff also all spoke to me in English, so I didn't manage to get much practise there either, even though we had agreed that they would help me in Arabic while working. It just turned out to be impractical, as I did not have enough of a basis to build upon.

Leading into the summer, the weather was getting a lot warmer, and our flat was lacking any air-conditioning. We decided to return to the UK to work during the summer then return to enroll in the more expensive, but hopefully more productive al-Fagr centre.

After working for a contract in the City, I took my family back to Cairo, rented our own apartment and started to work as a partner in a new company Reza, I and four Egyptians had just set up. We were developing web-sites for overseas clients. After I was settled again, I hunted around for Arabic classes. I tried Berlitz School for a few weeks, but found them to be very expensive. I then enrolled at al-Fagr. I managed to complete two full units, and was part way through my third.

Maajid, a mutual acquaintance of mine and Reza's from London, had started his compulsory year abroad as part of his Arabic and Law degree at SOAS in London. He was studying Arabic at the University of Alexandria, but he would occasionally travel to Cairo to meet with us and allow his wife a chance to meet some British friends and keep her sanity.

He was an active member of Hizb ut-Tahrir while at university in London, so possibly had either an Egyptian or British person inform the Egyptian State Security police (*Aman ad-Dawlah*) of his presence in Egypt. I had just returned from a weekend with our families at Maajid's flat in Alexandria, when we were all taken from our houses in the middle of the night.

Taken

When I had got back to my flat from Alexandria the day before, my house agent and neighbor Hisham told me of a police man who was asking questions about a foreigner who lived in this building. Hisham asked for ID, but when he showed it, he called his friend who is an officer in the police. The man then ran away, and we suspected that he was just trying to intimidate and blackmail a foreigner, so thought no more of it. He had accused me of running a vice ring upstairs, to which Hisham abused him and said it was absurd as he knew that my family was living there, and that we were modest people.

My family and I spent the evening at Reza's place then we returned home and all went to bed. My son, now two and a half, had been asleep for a while and I was just about to do the same, when a loud banging and continuous ringing of the doorbell prevented that. I found about 15 armed policemen lining the hallway and stairway up and up, together with two plain clothes men and a special forces officer. All the policemen were carrying rifles, and some had grenades. They asked for Medhat, whom I had never heard of, so I told them. They asked me who I was at the door and demanded to see ID.
I told them to wait while I got my passport. My Arabic was very poor at the time, but I could hear them saying "he's got a beard in the picture", which the other agreed to so they said that they were coming in.

They asked me who else was inside and then told me to wake my wife and get her into the living room. Initially some of the soldiers came inside, but after a short time they were sent out to wait in the hallway. Then one of the plain clothed officers asked to see my library, so I showed him my small number of books, most of which were in English or were my study books. He started to messily rummage through them, then wanted to see around the rest of the flat. He looked in wardrobes and under beds, but was not at all thorough in his search. I asked him what he was looking for and he just replied ominously "something special". I noticed that he took away any of my books that appeared to be about Islam in any way. He took about 26 in all.

Then he said that I have to come with him. He told me not to take any money but to bring my driver's licence and passport. My wife asked when I would be back, to which he replied "in about a week." We asked where I was going, and he said to the Khalifah police station.

He then escorted me in the lift to the waiting van outside. All of the soldiers had gone by now. On the way down he asked me if I knew of Hizb ut-Tahrir (HT)? I said "who doesn't, they are everywhere in the UK?" Then he asked me if I knew Reza? I said "which Reza, I know so many?" When we got to the van he said, "Oh I forgot your computer" So we went back up to get it. We entered to find my wife on the phone to Hisham, my housing agent, so the officer spoke to him briefly to say that I was being taken to the Khalifah police station. Then I hugged my wife and we left with my computer for the van.

The van stopped just around the corner, outside Reza's apartment building. All of the policemen, except a couple of guards, left to raid his place too. An hour or so later they came down with many bags of books and Reza. I greeted him solemnly as we started our journey to a place unknown. Reza pulled out a copy of the Qur'an and started to read it, and I wished that I had remembered to bring one too. On the way we each prayed our dawn (fajr) prayers in the van, which was far from clean, but had a piece of cardboard boxing on the floor apparently for that purpose. There was almost no conversation at all while in the van. We stopped at the flat our company had recently rented as offices and Reza was told to get out and open the door. They all returned later with seven computers.

Then we were taken to a small office in Cairo where all of our stuff was unloaded and we were taken to a room to confirm our names and nationalities. The plain clothes officers were laughing at us while there. I didn't yet know what to expect, but I was apprehensive.

We were then led into another van, where a man from Tajikistan was waiting, taken the same night. We were all then taken to a building which we later discovered was the State Security headquarters for Egypt, al-Gihaaz.

As we pulled into the courtyard we were blindfolded and led down some steps into a reception area. We joined a queue of others and were told to put our hands on the shoulders of the one in front. We filed to a desk, were asked our names, hand cuffed then led individually to cells. I was put into mine, told that I was number 26 then pushed down onto the concrete shelf that served as a bed. It had a disgustingly dirty thin mattress on it. I was told to sleep "*Nim!*", then the door banged closed behind me.

The cell was very cold and I was so glad that I had remembered to wear a sweater when they took me from my home. I hadn't yet slept at all and it was at least six in the morning, but I wasn't yet feeling tired. Adrenaline had been pumping through my veins for the past few hours and I was now high on it.

I started to think about my situation, about what could they want from me? What did they think they knew about me? What would happen next?

After about an hour, a man came calling numbers in succession, to which a person replied "*Aywah*?", then he would shout "*Qum*!" stand up. After a few seconds he'd shout "*Nim*!" When he reached my number he shouted "*Qum*!" I stood up, said "yes?" then tried to face the direction where his sound was coming from. I was still blindfolded and had my hands cuffed tightly behind my back. A man came into my cell and told me to sit down in English. I asked him for the British Consul to come and he said "No, don't worry you'll be deported after four days" then left.

I started to feel tired so tried to lie down and sleep a little.

Torture

I doubt if I actually slept. I was disturbed by the roll call of numbers and again stood when twenty six was called. This time the man just shouted "*Nim!*" telling me to sleep without opening the door. So I sat down again. This was to continue perhaps hourly for the rest of my time there.

At first, I daren't move between role calls, as I wasn't sure of the penalties for disobedience. I could hear breathing noises outside my cell door and I assumed that a guard had been made to sit there constantly checking on me. I gingerly started to explore my new environment during the periods between role calls. By now a small gap had appeared under my blindfold which allowed me to see downwards a little. I had to tip my head right back to see upwards, so I surveyed the room initially while lying on my back. I saw a hole-in-the-floor style toilet in the far corner, a tap next to it which ran straight onto the floor at about ankle height and not much else. The door was large and steel with a small window at about head height. This was the only source of light from the corridor. I was on a concrete bench which ran the length of the cell. The whole dimensions were about two metres by one and a half metres and about three metres high.

I wanted to use the toilet so I moved slowly and carefully. I thought that if they are watching me then they wouldn't be too hard on me if I was caught on the way to the toilet. I managed to turn on the tap by crouching and stretching my cuffed hands to one side so that they were almost in front of me. I drank water directly from the tap as I was now very thirsty.

After a period which I guessed to be about six hours I decided that it must be time to pray my midday prayer, so I slowly went to the tap and tried to wash myself. My hands could barely reach my face, so I had to wash it using just a couple of fingers with water on them. I stood up to pray, guessing the direction of Mecca. I was still conscious of the person outside of my door so I moved as quietly as possible. I wasn't able to put my hands down onto the floor when prostrating so I had to just do as much as I was able and pray that Allah forgives me due to my circumstances.

Now that I had succeeded in using the bathroom, drinking, washing and praying I felt very pleased. It was an almost liberating feeling; that I was not completely unable to have some control of my environment, and that I was not to be denied that thing that was now dearest to me, my prayer. It is inevitable, I think, that when a person is completely alone in his suffering, then he will turn to what gives him solace. Prayer was the best way I knew how to get closer to my Lord and ask for his help.

Twice a day the guard would come to my cell, unlock the door and tell me to turn around so that he could unlock my cuffs and move them to the front. He gave me a hurried swig from a bottle of water, then left me with a sandwich in my hand. It was a folded piece of Egyptian flat round bread, filled with rice and a piece of chicken. In the mornings he came with *halawa* (sunflower seed and sugar paste) and cheese in the sandwich. The alternate foods for breakfast and dinner gave me clues to guess what time of day it was outside. The chicken was so dry and was filled with bones, but I still ate most of it. I discovered that a previous occupant of my cell had used the foot of the bench to throw the bones, so I did likewise. Ironically, I was to discover in a few days that this was extremely good food when compared to that which is served in the prisons. After about an hour he came back to return my cuffs to the back.

Later on the first day, during one of the role calls, I was told to come out of my cell and sit in the corridor. Then other prisoners who had been waiting in the corridor were led one at a time into my cell to use the toilet in there. When I had used it myself it turned out to be quite a messy experience, as I tried to balance in a crouched position with my hands behind my back. By the smell when I was returned to the cell, I could tell that the others had just as much difficulty as me. I then discovered that the thin mattress had been removed and was now being used by the other prisoners sitting in the corridor.

My handcuffs were behind my back so I tried to lie on my back, but the cuffs dug into my back. I tried on my side but my arm went numb. I tried on my front, but then my face was into the cold concrete. I eventually took off my shoes and placed them under my backside to raise myself higher than my cuffs and so relieve the pressure a little. Even this position I could only sustain for a short while though. I then took to moving my shoes with my teeth into a pillow like position then lying on my side for as long as I could. After that I would just alternate between all of these positions in a futile attempt to find some lasting comfort in that very uncomfortable place. Prolonged discomfort, after all, was another of their intimidation and mistreatment techniques.

By now the cell had become very cold. I could hear the constant hum from the corridor of the air conditioning machine and was particularly aware of it when the power cut a couple of times. The room became noticeably warmer after only about half an hour without the air conditioning machine, but when the power came back then it became very cold again. I suspect that they had the control set to maximum refrigeration to further make our situation more uncomfortable.

I wasn't able to sleep, nor was I feeling particularly tired at the time, and I wasn't able to pray continuously, so I started to revise what little of the Qur'an I had memorised up to that point. Regrettably I had only about 120 verses committed to memory, mostly from the short chapters at the end of the Qur'an and a few pages from the third chapter, Aal-Imraan. Still, I searched through what I had, trying to find something to give me strength. At that stage my understanding of Arabic was still quite weak, so many of the words used in what I was revising had little meaning for me. I was able to go through the Arabic grammar rules related to each word (*i'raab*), to know its role in the sentence, but the detailed meaning was unknown to me. How I regretted this.

On the second day I became more daring in my movements. I wanted to pray properly with my hands on my chest, so I remembered how it is possible to step backwards through your joined hands to achieve this. The cuffs were so tight at first, that pulling them over my backside was too painful, and I was also afraid that if I did it then I wouldn't be able to get them back again. I thought of excuses to say if I got caught with them in the front: "the guard forgot to return them last time I was fed". Anyway, I finally did bring them forward and felt very pleased with myself.

It was another small victory of defiance and a refusal to accept my current situation as I exercised what little control I still had. I discovered that bringing them back was much easier.

For the rest of my time in the cell, I would bring my hands to the front to loosen my blindfold and sometimes even remove it. Prior to this, I had been able to roll it up by rubbing my face against the bench, but getting it back when a role call started was much more difficult. Now, I still replaced my blindfold and brought my hands to the back when I heard the roll call, but with significantly more ease and swiftness. I nearly got caught once, panicking me a little, but other than that I was very fortunate.

Throughout those first two days I would hear the regular screams from down the hall. They started on the evening of my first night there, continued throughout the night then died down by the morning, until the next evening. It was another way for me to guess the time of day. The screams seemed far away, but their reality was very close, as I could hear the numbers being called, then a door opening, then the screams starting again shortly afterwards. This may go on for half an hour or so, before another number was called out. The place was like a factory, a conveyor belt of torture. I could hear one man's name called an awful lot. He was called Shareef, and I was afraid that it was a friend of mine from the village, also called Shareef.
He used to talk to me in English, as he was a student of English literature. My whole family had dined at his house when they had visited me in my flat in Cairo. I was afraid that he had been brought in for associating with me. Not a pleasant thought. It turned out that he had not been arrested, but I didn't know that until about two months later.

The screams were blood curdling. Grown men's high pitch screams preceded by a buzzing and crackling sound. They would sometimes shout some words, but I couldn't understand them. I imagined that they had a machine which a person was strapped into, then the voltage was applied to produce the screams I could hear. The reality was much more crude, as I discovered from conversations with prisoners more than a year later. Most people were stripped down to their underwear, forced onto the floor, then a wooden chair was placed in top of their legs. A guard sat on the chair then a cattle-prod-like device was placed on their leg to create a current which left through their feet. Their body would spasm with the shock and normally they would defecate and urinate themselves as their bodies lost control. This would continue for about twenty minutes, then they'd be led to the shower room to clean up and get dressed. Some had wires attached to their genitalia before electricity was turned on. Others were stabbed, had acid poured down their backs (I saw the marks), nearly drowned then live wires would be put into the water.

Many captives from our case had their hands tied behind their backs with electrical wire then they were hung from it on the top of an open door, almost as if they were carcasses in a butcher's waiting to be cut up. They would be left like this sometimes for hours. The wire cut into their skin only making the already agonising experience even more excruciating.

I occasionally heard the guards walk past my cell and with them I would hear the crackling and buzzing of the torture stick they were holding. I shivered as I wondered when my own turn would be.

Interrogation

On the third day after being taken from my house, the guard led me from my cell to an office where I was told to stand in front of a desk. A man was standing to my left. I could only see downwards through the gap between the now loose blindfold and my face. I could see his shoes, which were light grey leather slip-ons, and his trousers, which looked equally cheap. When he spoke he had a voice that betrayed years of chain smoking, so I guessed him to be in his fifties. I could sense that he was a small, ugly old man. At the desk was a man sitting whose voice told me he was much younger. I never saw his shoes or trousers, as they were hidden by the desk. There were others in the room, but seemed to be more observers than active participants.

The room was well lit, had tiled floors, wooden chairs and huge metal desks, straight out of the seventies. It wasn't as cold in there.

The sitting man started to question me about who I was, why I was in Egypt, where I lived and studied etc. all very innocuous. Everything I said, he was taking notes in pencil on sheets of lined paper on the desk. After some time I was told to sit on a wooden chair in front of the desk. Then came the more probing questions.

The man behind the desk could speak only broken English and I only broken Arabic, so there were frequent moments when I could not understand the question and he had to find another way of asking it.

They asked me about my relationship with Hizb ut-Tahrir, but I didn't want to talk about that, so I emphasised that I was just studying Arabic in Egypt. I tried to be vague whenever they asked me anything, as I wasn't sure of how things could get worse if I said the wrong thing.

They asked me about the books that they had taken from my flat. The State Security officer who took me had found my spare room with about fifty Islamic books in it. Mostly collections of Hadith (sayings of the Prophet (saw)) or books of law. They all belonged to Maajid who had bought them at the Cairo book fair in February and was storing them before shipping them home to London. He had asked me about them, so I said they belonged to a friend. The interrogator behind the desk asked me who the friend was. I wasn't aware that Maajid had been arrested yet, so I decided that I would not mention him, as I didn't want them to send out police to raid his flat as well. Not knowing how much they know puts you in a very weak position. I wanted to come across believable, yet at the same time not to give them anything they hadn't already got.

Whilst I may end up incriminating myself, I certainly did not want to be the cause of anyone else being taken and tortured. This was the limit that I had established mentally while in the cell. It was an extremely stressful situation.

They wanted to know who the friend was, so I said Kashif, Maajid's brother, who had recently visited Cairo, but I knew to be home safely far away from Egypt right at that moment. I reasoned that the lie was necessary to protect a friend's identity. I chose Kashif because I wanted something that was close enough to the truth, that I would remember it easily, but not too close that it causes any trouble. Then came a whole torrent of questions about Kashif. Where was he from, how did I know him, where was he now, what was his connection to HT? etc. etc. I did not want to give away much information about him either, as I wasn't sure where it would lead to. I was also conscious that lies always get you in deeper trouble, as they soon get exposed by contradictions in the story.

The officer started to get angry that I wasn't forthcoming in my approach; giving him only brief answers in response to his questions. I agreed to his request for me speak more without being questioned, but nothing actually changed.

To these officers all people who want to see Islam implemented are backward. They have been brought up on a diet of lies about Muslims who call for the return of Islam, even though they call themselves Muslims. Egypt has had its violent civil war with Islamist groups wanting to overthrow the government, so they think that they have seen it all. We are all tarred with the same brush. So, when they accused me of *takfir* (calling the Egyptian people non-Muslims) I felt that I had to break down this misconception of theirs. It is true that many of those who fought the government did look down upon the Egyptian people and pronounce them all to be non-believers, yet this is not my view, nor the orthodox mainstream Sunni view. I wanted to show these officers that they don't know it all and that people like me are not the enemy. Also, I wanted to emphasise that I do not support the violent struggle for change and that reform of ideas is all that I believe in. I got my point across, but whether it fell on deaf ears, only Allah knows.

They asked me which Egyptians I knew, so I had to be so vague, avoiding answering in any way that would lead to them harassing my friends and neighbours. I said I didn't know him whenever they suggested a name that they felt I should have known.

At this point the short old man with the cheap shoes flew into a rage screaming at me in unintelligible Egyptian, I feel sure that he was spitting while speaking. He pushed me against the wall. He started to punch me and poke me in the body and face. I was still blindfolded and cuffed. He taunted me as he saw the shock on my face. He was screaming on in Egyptian, but I had no idea what he was saying. He threw a glass on floor where it smashed at my feet. He then dragged me onto the floor forcing me to kneel in front of him while he sat on the wooden chair. He asked me in calmer Egyptian where my wife and son were? *"fayn zugtuk wa ibnuk?"* Did I know that she was safe? I could just understand the Arabic, but I clearly saw what he was saying. He carried on threatening my family, then returned me to my seat.

Now they wanted to know about my past in England, how I became Muslim, who invited me and so on. This was easier to talk about and it was using the vocabulary that I had been recently studying on my course. Again they asked me about the books in my flat and about Kashif. This time, they slyly asked me who Maajid was. I was taken aback that they knew of him, and again I didn't know how much they knew. I quickly calculated that they may have somebody in custody who knew Maajid, so answered vaguely that he is a friend in the UK.

They told me that they knew the books in my flat were for Maajid, and I could sense their glee that they had caught me out, but I replied "yes, Maajid is Kashif's brother". Those in the room laughed and commented something like "this one is clever (*mahir*)."

I was taken back into my cell. My head was spinning from what I had just been through. I was relieved that I could now rest, but I could feel the stress as I tried to remember how I had answered their questions, so that if I was questioned again I could answer the same. The intensity of the situation did not really lessen and, not surprisingly, I wasn't able to properly relax. It was now the third night and I had had only a few short snatches of sleep during my ordeal. I could now hear the screams continuing down the corridor.

Later on that night I was taken back into the same office with the same people in it. Now came a new set of accusations that I was expected to submit to. I was told that they had an email about me from an Egyptian member of Hizb ut-Tahrir which stated that I had been sent by HT in the UK to Egypt. This I knew to be false, so I was sure it was a fishing expedition on their part. They only became harsher whenever I denied any of their accusations. I was now beginning to see that they aren't really interested in establishing any facts during this interrogation. They were more interested in filling in any gaps with their own assumptions, then forcing you to agree and accept their version of the reality as true.

I feel that their arrogance has led them to believe in their own powers of deduction; so much so that they become convinced of their own hypotheses. It does not matter the lies and coercion that they have to use to get someone to admit to their hypotheses; that he admits is all important and proof that they were right all along. I suspect that they are under enormous pressure from their bosses to quickly produce consistent stories that do not contain errors, so the real truth becomes unimportant, and their truth must now prevail.

They sat me down again and this time asked me about an email that I had apparently given to an Egyptian. It allegedly contained twelve names of Egyptians who had met HT in the UK. I again knew that there was no such email, so I denied it. They repeated the question a few times, so I carried on denying it.

Cheap shoes stepped aggressively to me and started his usually unintelligible rant. I could tell that he was asking me many questions, waiting for my response, pushing me, but I couldn't answer, as I didn't know what he was asking. This went on for a while with the tension rising until finally I shouted back in exasperation "what do you want, I can't understand your question". This tickled those in the room, so the man became calmer, asking me something about hearing and how long I have been here. Maybe one of the others said a few words in English to help me, but it suddenly dawned on me what exactly he was saying.

He was asking me about the screams that I had heard during my time in their dungeon; what do I think was causing them? Did I want some of the same?

This was it then. This was when they would unleash their animals with the electricity shocking machine. They led me to a new room around the corner and made me stand in the doorway. I could see a tiled floor with some people wearing shoes and trousers. I could also see a man with bare feet in the middle. They asked him some questions and he replied desperately to them. He kept saying "*effendi*" which is like saying sir. He was obviously pleading with them not to hurt him anymore. In their questions I heard the words "email" and "*itnaashar ism*" twelve names. He replied "*Aywa*" yes "*itnaashar ism*" in confirmation. I was then sat down in the doorway with my back turned. I heard the buzzing and crackling of the torture machine and then the man's screams as they put it onto him. He was severely being tortured because of what I was saying. It was due to the inconsistency in his acceptance of their story and my denial. This fact tore me apart inside. I could grit my teeth and try to prepare for my own mistreatment, but having another innocent person being tortured immediately based upon my own words weakened me incredibly. The link between me and his suffering was too explicit, too immediate. I was now confused and wanted only to end this situation. I started to feel that resistance to their accusations was futile.

After seeing what he was willing to do to end the suffering, I felt pressured to not make him out to be a liar in their eyes anymore. Looking back I can see that it makes little difference to the investigation whether you oppose them or cooperate with them. The results are just a shambled mix of lies and half truths anyway; but at the time it was much harder to look at it like that. Quick decisions had to be made.

After a while I was taken back into the office, asked again about the email and its twelve names, and this time I replied that I did have such an email. They asked me for the names but I replied that I didn't remember them as they were all on the email not in my head. I sensed their happiness that they had gotten to 'the truth' with me, so the interrogation ended for that day and I was led back into my cell.

I had never really prepared for such a situation. I knew that the Egyptian government persecuted anyone who stood up against their oppression, particularly Islamists. As a member of HT from the UK I was obviously aware of the hatred that they had for my ideas, but I thought it unlikely that they would ever know who I was, let alone actually do anything about it.

To my knowledge Hizb-ut-Tahrir in Egypt was still very underground and not much in the public-eye, hence I would not be very actively pursued, or so I thought. Had I read more about other people's accounts of similar circumstances I feel that it would have allowed me to mentally prepare myself in advance. The uncertainty of what to expect is the torturer's best weapon, as he plays upon that to further intimidate. By knowing his limits, one is able to estimate when he is bluffing. Knowing his technique is half way to knowing how to deal with it. Staying focused is everything, but very difficult to do. Later I would have discussions with fellow prisoners who had been through worse than I had, but they confirmed through their anecdotes that the investigating officers only half believe everything they hear. They know that people will agree to anything to stop the pain of torture. As the pain becomes worse or the threat of the severity of the torture becomes more real, then the victim becomes more and more intimidated until he says anything in a desperate attempt to stop it.

The next time I was taken into the interrogation room, was on the fourth day of my imprisonment. The investigating officer spoke to me in clear English with an American accent. He said that he had been brought in especially to interview me due to the difficulties in communication of the day before. He was more relaxed than the other officers were, but then he knew that he didn't have to put any more pressure on me to play their game.

He covered all the same ground as yesterday regarding myself and why I was in Egypt. He loosened my blindfold slightly at one point as he wanted me to write my email address details down on a piece of paper. I knew that he'd just find a few personal emails and a load of spam, but it kept him happy.

After that, for the rest of the day, he just asked me lots of questions about how I became a Muslim, who invited me, who did I know in the UK. It was all irrelevant information, but I was still vague about peoples' names. I often just chose a name from a highly public personality rather than someone that they don't already know of. I was shocked that they mentioned a name of an Egyptian whom I had met once at university in the UK. I was later able to smuggle this information to him to warn him of the danger he is in if he returned to Egypt. I have heard that he was granted Asylum in Britain based upon this information.

The interrogator became annoyed with me for not being pro-active, but just answering his questions. I agreed to be more forthcoming, but just continued to answer him as before. Strangely, I felt more at ease on this second day of my interrogation. I think that I felt more secure due to my decision to implicate myself the previous day. It was almost as if now they were just going through a formality that didn't really matter, as they already had enough to make a case against me.

I didn't understand the judicial system in Egypt at the time, so I considered that his notes would be read out in court against me just as a policeman's notes are read out in the UK. Prior to that I was trying to stay alive and get out of there without saying anything to make matters worse. Now, matters were already worse, so I just concentrated on staying alive.

We continued with my biography, not reaching much more than when I joined HT. Then I was sent to sit in the hallway for a while. My hands were cuffed to my front and I was given a cup of tea. It was the best thing that I had tasted for days, and the caffeine had a wonderful effect in a tired body. I had still only caught glimpses of sleep from the hourly roll-call and also the stress of rehearsing my answers over and over. I realised that if I was to be believed in my answers then they had to be consistent. I knew I had to keep completely made up answers to the minimum lest I get confused and hesitate too much while answering. The trick was to try to find out how much they already knew before mentioning any more details. It becomes more difficult when they are questioning more than one person, as you don't know what that other person has said, and you need to be consistent with him too. Any discrepancies should appear as mere errors and not attempts to lie. This is what was going through my mind, so preventing my sleep in between the screams and guard's shouts.

While I was in the corridor I heard Maajid's voice telling the guards that they had the wrong Mahmood; that the one they had taken from Alexandria wasn't then one they thought he was. Then I saw his shoes as he was led past me. Now I knew that it wasn't just Reza, me and some unknown Egyptians in there, but that they had virtually everyone I knew in Egypt. Another shock!

After a short time I was taken into a different office to resume my life story, still in the UK. They were never interested in asking me many questions about Egypt. There was a window open in that room. I could hear the noise from up high by the ceiling so I knew that we were underground in the basement. I had become a little more adventurous in surveying my surroundings as I discovered ways to take peeps which appeared to be just flinches or innocent movements. When the *adhan* called from a nearby mosque I could hear it inside. It gave me another clue as to what time of day it was. I guessed it to be midday to early afternoon. I was surprised that the officer mentioned to the other next to him that he was off to pray. I asked if I could pray too, so they agreed and led me back to my cell. My blindfold was taken off me and the handcuffs removed for the first time in four days.

After our prayers I was led back to the same room, now cuffed and blindfolded again. Before he started his questions again I asked him how it is that he could pray to Allah while at the same time torture us? He sounded shocked and said "did anyone shock you with electricity?" I said "no", so he replied coldly, "those are bad people".

Before long, some people came into the room, spoke briefly to the interrogator in Egyptian, then I was hurriedly led away. I was led out of a gate then shoved into a prisoners transport van while one hand was cuffed to a guard. The van drove off, up a slope and onto Cairo's busy streets. Civilisation at last! We hadn't travelled more than a few hundred metres when the guards removed my blindfold and undid the handcuffs. It was dark outside, but street lights gave enough light to see who was in there with me. I was overjoyed to see Reza, Maajid in there with me. I was surprised to see Hussein, Abdul Azim and the Tajeki man there too. Hussein was an English student at Maajid's university in Alexandria whom I had met a few times. Abdul Azim was also a student there and a Japanese convert to Islam, who had no English, so I hardly knew him. He shared a flat with Hussein both communicating in a mixture of Arabic, Japanese and English, impenetrable to anyone else, dubbed *Lugha Hussein* (Hussein's language).

This was the first time that we had spoken for days. I heard that Reza had been shocked with electricity but that the rest of us hadn't. It upset me to think of a friend suffering. I think I kissed him on the cheek and prayed that he be rewarded for his suffering. The shock of what had been happening and the confusion I felt cannot be described easily. I remember that I didn't want to hear how the others had answered the questions as I didn't want to overhear anything that I didn't already know. I was afraid of getting more confused and of possibly blurting out something harmful if tortured myself. Regardless of whether you are a criminal or not in that place, you're made to feel like one. Even the most innocuous mention of a name comes back to haunt you, as you then become the master conspirator in a great secret plan. Those State Security officers are seriously paranoid people, capturing and torturing people based solely on their associations, even chance encounters. They cannot be wrong ever, so every capture must be justified.

As we drove along the streets, we appeared to be heading in the direction of the airport. Maajid speculated that we would be deported most likely.

Prosecutor

We soon were disappointed as we arrived at another large building filled with police. We didn't know where we were. We were led upstairs to wait in an empty corridor. Our handcuffs were now removed. After maybe four hours of sitting and talking amongst ourselves, we were lined up and led one by one into an office. He was a head prosecutor, but I didn't know it at the time. On my turn, he just asked my name, filled some paper, then I was led out back to the hallway. Was this just a deportation formality?

No, this was the beginning of our investigation. The past four days hadn't actually taken place. There is no torture in Egyptian police stations, or so the official line goes. Everyone who confesses to a crime does so voluntarily either in the police van (not coerced of course) or at the prosecutor's desk where he is overcome with guilt. I used to laugh at a daily Egyptian newspaper's section called "Red Handed" where every day they printed a story of a criminal who spontaneously confessed to his crime. They must have a lot of guilty consciences in Egypt.

Torture is so common and so well known about in Egypt. It is just outside of Egypt that we tend to be unaware of our favourite holiday host's brutality.
A popular Egyptian joke tells of how archaeologists discovered a new Pharonic era statue, but had no information about who it was. A Ministry of the Interior official offered to help find out. Two days later he returned saying that it is Ramses III. They asked amazed "how do you know?" to which the official replied "he confessed".

Abdul Azim, the Japanese man, and the Tajeki were taken away and we never saw either again. The remaining four British were left in the corridor until we were each taken into separate offices to talk to the head prosecutors. I still did not know who I was talking to. For me it was just a continuation of what I had been through before, but without the blindfold. I strongly believed that I would be returned back to the torturers later that night. The interrogation started more-or-less where the other had left off, and I could see that the prosecutor was reading from the same penciled notes that the torturer had made earlier.

In the room with me were a scribe, an interpreter and the prosecutor. He would ask me a question then the interpreter would ask me in English. I would answer then that would be relayed back to the prosecutor. He would then dictate an answer to the scribe who scribbled it down. To this day I don't know exactly what my official "confession" said. I could tell that some of my answers were being horribly distorted and abbreviated, even with my limited Arabic.

I have only heard a summarised version of what was presented to the court, which I hardly recognised.

I asked to see a lawyer and the British Consul before answering any questions, but I was told that they have been contacted and are not interested in coming to see you. It was made very clear to me that even though my blindfold was no longer on, my situation was no less dire than earlier that day. I could see the prosecutor reading from the same pencil written notes that the torturer had written during my earlier interrogation. He would frequently be on the phone or walk out of the room to confer with one of his colleagues during the night. He also had a book called "Hizb-ut-Tahrir" which he would refer to when asking questions and deciding what to write into my "confession".

Occasionally he would stop the scribe to ask me off-the-record questions, such as "why do you want to see change in Egypt?" It was no less than taunting me to be asked what was wrong with what I had just been witness to. How can any person see such oppression and not want it to change?!!

When we had come to the end of the session that night, after about four hours of questioning, he gave me some food and a drink, then told me to sign the "confession" papers.
Initially I refused, and he became visibly angry. Again I was reminded that I could easily be going back to the torture place that I had just come from. I reluctantly signed the papers. I considered putting a wrong signature on the paper, but I could see that he had my passport on his desk to check against. Later I heard how Reza had signed his "confession" with a signature that spelt out "lies" and "hurt" in them. He had gambled that they would be clear to any British person to read, but would go unnoticed by the Egyptians. He was right. I wished that I had thought of doing that as well, but I was too confused and tired by now.

After all was wrapped up for the evening, and he had his signature, he told me that he was a prosecutor and that this was an official investigation to establish whether any crime had been done. Until that moment I had not realised where I was and I suddenly regretted signing the paper, as now I realised that this could actually be used in court to incriminate me. His name was Muhammad Qandeel he told me. He used to travel to London for heart treatment in Magdi Yaqub's clinic. He said that he'd be going again soon, and would I like anything to be brought back? More taunting.

After the Prosecutor had left the room and there was only myself, the interpreter and the scribe in the room, the interpreter, who was by now visibly shaken, told me of his shock that I was being put through this ordeal. He looked scared, as he worked for the television company and was not used to dealing with State Security. He and the scribe both said that they could not see that I had done anything wrong based upon the questions being asked and my answers, and they felt that it was unjust that I even be there.

When the prosecutor returned, he asked me if I wanted to call my family. I did not know what had happened to them for five days now, so I said yes. I dialed the flat number from his desk, but there was no answer. I then tried Reza's home number and got through to Reza's wife. I asked if she knew where my wife was and she called her to the phone. I told her that I was in the prosecutor's office and then I asked if she was safe? The prosecutor heard the word safe and asked me who is he? Safe is a man's name in Egypt. I told him what I had really asked and he was OK with that. I answered a few of her questions about my treatment, then I said to my wife that it is best for her to go and stay with her father, whom I knew to be in London. She got the message, *Alhamdulillah*.

Then the four of us were taken in a van at dawn to the Tora prison complex. It was a large walled area with many guards, barracks, prisons and farm land in it. We drove about half a mile into the complex then stopped outside Mazra'a Tora prison. It would be our home for the next four years.

Prison

Our first four months were spent in the punishment cells on cell block two. They were bare individual cells about 4 metres high, two metres wide and 2.5 metres long. The roof had a rectangular barred hole and there was a barred opening for a window above the heavy steel door. The walls were over one metre thick and made from stone blocks held together with cement. There was a crumbling layer of plaster on the inside. The floor was bare concrete. There was no toilet or tap.

My first night was on that floor with only me and a bottle of tap water in the cell. I was so tired after five days without sleep that I just collapsed, using the bottle as a pillow and slept. The next day we were brought a blanket each, then a few days later a few more blankets. I had three underneath me and one on top. Egyptian prison blankets are made from the most tough grey wool I'd ever seen. They were filled with bugs and dirt, so I got bitten a lot.

I was allowed to use the bathroom on the first afternoon, Friday. It was a disgusting hole in the ground in an adjacent cell. I had a tap in the courtyard to wash my hands and face. Our own filthy clothes were taken away from us and replaced by tatty prison issue clothing.

It consisted of cotton pyjama-like trousers with a weak elastic waist, and a rough cotton shirt whose three buttons did not line up. On the back was written "*masjoon*" Prisoner. Our clothes were white, as we were still under investigation. Later an officer came to ask if we wanted anything, so I immediately thought "toothbrush and paste". After all I had been through the most important thing I could think of was as mundane as a toothbrush. He brought us one each (a couple of them did not look new) and we all smiled at each other as we did our teeth. A few years later I would read the book 'A long walk' by S. Rawicz about his imprisonment and escape in wartime Russia. He recalled in it his excitement at being given his first coat after weeks of marching in the winter. He also mentioned how he and the other prisoners joked about how good they looked in their new coats; bizarre considering the circumstances. But I identified with that as I remembered my own brushed teeth.

We were locked up and isolated from each other for the first few weeks, except when taking us to the prosecutor's office during the night. I was taken on four consecutive nights. Generally we went in the same van, but once we went in separate vans with a guard each handcuffed to our wrists. One time they blindfolded me again and made me march around the van and into the building; a pointless exercise in intimidation.

On the last day of my prosecution sessions, once all of the papers of my 'confession' were signed and complete, I was again allowed to phone my wife, this time to the UK. When I spoke to her, I was relieved that she was safe at her father's home. I tried to pass a discrete message about the use of electricity here, but I couldn't make myself understood without being too explicit. I tried it in the Urdu words that Maajid had just taught me, but my message wasn't very clear. I had to be careful as the interpreter was still being requested to translate all that I was saying.

On the first Friday, the prison governor (*ma'moor*) came to visit us and ask us if we wanted anything. He arranged for a couple of extra blankets each, as the night time was still quite cold in April.

During the days, after the prosecutor's investigation, I was left in my cell with nothing to do. I had managed to get a newspaper from a guard at the prosecutor's office, but it was an Arabic copy of al-Ahram which I couldn't read yet. I started to practice making paper boats etc. I also made up a game where I would flick small pieces of paper into an empty bowl once I'd eaten my dinner. I found a rusty nail on my cell floor, so I used it to scratch into the steel door. I practiced long division, which was always my weakness at university.

British Consul

On the eleventh day of our imprisonment, after all of the prosecutor's 'investigation' was completed and our 'confessions' had been signed, the British Consul came to visit the four of us.

We were taken from our cells and led out of the punishment cells to a laundry room. The officer escorting us ordered some prisoners to give us new prison clothes to replace the grotty rags that we were wearing. Cosmetics for the Consul's benefit. We were then escorted to the office of the governor (*ma'moor*) of the prison. It was a large room with a verse from the Qur'an painted in huge letters on the wall. I saw many men, some wearing dark glasses in casual clothes; obviously State Security. Others were officers in uniform and then I saw the British Consul Gordon Brown and his vice-Consul, Andy.

After greeting us solemnly the vice Consul spoke to Hussein and I. He asked us about who we were, and whether we had any connection to HT in the UK. Then he asked if we had been tortured or mistreated. We spoke in hushed tones as we described the treatment that we had been subjected to. I complained about our current situation; our denial of access to the toilet, our bare cells and the isolation, as well as my investigation and lack of access to a lawyer or the Consul until now.
While I was complaining about our poor living conditions, Andy saw fit to remind me that I was prisoner and that "it's not a hotel that you're staying in", as if I needed reminding of that.

Reza's mother, who lived in Cairo, had sent in some soap, towels and packets of "Bachelor's Cuppa-Soup" with the Consul. A few hours after we returned to our cells, these were sent through to us. Finally I could add some flavour to my bland food. The prison food was so flavourless that I had began to crave for salt. In its absence, however, I was now able to sprinkle on top the tomato soup powder.

That night, we were woken in the middle of the night then taken handcuffed and blindfolded again into the offices of the prison's management block. I was taken into the *ma'moor*'s office where I had been sitting with the Consul earlier that day. Then I heard the voice of the same State Security investigator that I recognised from the torture chambers, al-Gihaaz. He explained that he had come back to complete his investigation. He wanted my computer account details again so that he could check my messages. He also wanted to repeat a lot of the same questions as before. After a couple of hours they were gone and I was back in my cold bare cell. It was a clear message: "you may well complain to the British Consul, but you're with us and we can do as we like with you".

Punishment Cells

After a week or so, the guard allowed us each one hour outside of the cell. We had a small courtyard with bars over our heads and rubble on the floor. I wasn't allowed to talk to the others through their cell doors at first, but this was relaxed later. Later still, they allowed us our hour at the same time, and then it grew by two hours, then to two hours from ten until twelve, then two more from two until four. It remained like that for about a month.

After a while we were given an Arabic Qur'an each in response to our request, then we were given an English novel each. Unknown to us there was an American citizen in the prison, whose Consul would occasionally deliver books. The State Security officer took them from him, but told us that he'd gone out to get these especially for us.

For most of our time in the isolation block, perhaps the first three months there, we were not allowed to use the bathroom after lockup at 6pm. Despite our repeated requests, we were continuously denied. We were told to use our cell floors, which I did have to do on one occasion early on. I had only one bottle for drinking water and no other container to urinate in. I was forced to use the corner of my cell. I could still smell the stench after four months when I left the cell.

After that, I acquired a spare bottle. Generally I was forced to prevent myself from doing number two except when I could hold it no more. I had to use a thin carrier bag, which is an extremely unpleasant experience. In the morning, at 8am when our doors were opened, there would be a queue as we all rushed to use the bathroom.

We complained to the Consul repeatedly about this most basic of human rights and the Egyptian prison authority's contentious violation of it. Each time the Consul would raise it with the *ma'moor* who would then invent yet another new excuse to justify his refusal. It usually ended with, "we'll see what we can do", which translated as "wait until the morning". A favourite excuse was that the keys for our cells were kept outside of the prison grounds and so it was impossible to open then at night-time at all. The ridiculousness of this lie was evident as we were taken to the prosecutor's office at night every two weeks. We later learned that all of the prison's keys are kept in a box in the management block and can be accessed at anytime by the duty officer. Indeed, after three months they finally relented and made a final nightly round with a key at 10pm offering us the chance to use the bathroom. As it was now July, with temperatures of up to 37 degrees in the cell at night, I would have a quick shower to cool down then return to try to sleep.

During July 2002 was the world cup in Japan and Seoul. The prison authorities, in an act of pacification, turned up one day with a TV and someone to fit an aerial on our roof. They provided a long cable so that it could be moved from cell to cell allowing us one evening in four to watch the football. I have never been a football fan, only supporting whichever team's kit I had been handed down as a child (I swapped from Chelsea to Manchester United to Liverpool). I never watched any of the games though, just preferring to play the game at school or occasionally with my friends. I did make an exception for the World Cup. I can remember my sister and I watching in horror as Maridonna pushed the ball into the goal with his hand in 1986. Anyway, the 2002 world cup was the first time I had followed the entire tournament, and it certainly broke the monotony of isolation block prison life. As we now had electricity in our cells, we could have lights at night for the first time, and we were even given a fan each; a huge relief during Egyptian summer nights. I did not need a lamp as I had had continuous near daylight in my cell for the past three months. A huge spotlight was pointing into my cell's window making it very difficult to sleep. I missed the dark and was probably the only happy person in Cairo whenever there was a power-cut.

Sometime during the first month I received my first letter from home. My wife and parents had written a short note to let me know that they were praying for me and that they would do whatever they could to help. I had never doubted that they would, but I was extremely glad to read those words all the same. Even a little communication settled my restless heart, as it brought such comfort to know that my loved ones were with me.

All our letters from the prison were screened at first, with sections occasionally crossed out. A fellow prisoner from the criminal wing who had excellent English was brought to summarise for the State Security officer all incoming and outgoing correspondence. He was even asked to sit in on our early visits, although we made it very clear that this we would not tolerate. If we wanted to get a message out to our families about our case, then we had to either wait until a family visit, or on a court hearing day, we could scribble a note and pass it through the mesh of the cage. By the end of our trial, interest in our letters had dwindled significantly, so letters came in and out much more quickly. I generally tried to send at least one letter per week, to leave with the driver who brought our food delivery. Whenever I received a letter I was very excited. Any news of my family was very welcome. In a place where there is so little news, where even dreams become important news bulletins, it is hard not to share stories from back home with my friends.

I had calculated that if you spend a year with someone, every day walking and discussing your lives, you get to know them so well that actually you run out of past stories to tell. You reach a state of contentment of just sharing each other's company, without the need for conversation. However, when news does arrive, it is lovely to share it with people who are almost as interested to hear it as yourself.

While still in the punishment block we were forced to eat the prison food. Each day had one delivery of a dish of either watery lentils, watery beans, weakly flavoured courgettes or oily broad beans. All served with rice, stones and occasional insects. In the morning three pieces of flat Egyptian bread were delivered to us along with a piece of salty cheese and a small tub of *halawa* (sunflower seed paste and sugar). Breakfast was by far the better meal. Surprisingly I only became violently ill on one occasion, and that was after three months.

The courtyard wasn't long enough to do any serious exercise, but we managed to invent a cross-training system of short sprints, sit-ups and weight lifting using each other and the guard's bench. We had now gained a floor-mat each which we would bring out into the courtyard to sit on and eat, read or exercise together. One of the guards had climbed on top of our cage to tie a couple of blankets to create a shaded area from the sun.

One day a prisoner came up to the courtyard door, lifted the metal flap covering the small window and called one of us over. He said that he was British just like us, "do you know what I mean?" in a heavy Egyptian accent. I thought it was some dodgy spying attempt, but he later became a friend, once I got to know him.

It was near to the end of July before they opened the courtyard door to allow us into the rest of the prison.

Investigation

For four months after we were taken from our homes, we had to attend the prosecutor's office every fifteen days. On one of these trips, after maybe four weeks, we were crammed into a van with our guards cuffed to us. There we found it full with Egyptians from our case. They were being held at the neighbouring prison, Istiqbaal. They were kept in two large cells, all 114 of them. Their situation was more cramped than ours, but they weren't kept in the same isolation. I recognised a couple of the men from Alexandria, who were Maajid's friends from his University, but other than that the van was mostly strangers. The summer was starting so the van become increasingly hotter as the day wore on.

Our journey was about one hour in the van which can only be described as a steel box on wheels. It had six small windows with bars and steel mesh covering them. If I stood with my mouth pressed against the bars, fresh air could be breathed when the van was moving. With only enough room for two people at each window, most of us had to do with the hot, humid, stale air in the van. We were about thirty prisoners along with ten guards inside of the van. We had no handles to hold onto, so just held onto each other. Whenever the driver braked, we all lurched forward; sometimes falling and getting hurt.

I get travel sick on London buses, so those journeys were particularly harrowing for me. The floor was just a steel plate, often covered in the urine of the van's previous inhabitants.

You'd think we'd all be very miserable in those conditions. When we got into the van, we were greeted like long lost relatives. Each person wanted to shake our hand and kiss us on each cheek, a standard warm Egyptian greeting. As we were travelling, someone would start to sing a song (called a *nasheed*). They weren't pop songs, but more traditional Islamic folk songs. Not knowing the words I just listened at first, but after a few journeys like that, I even started to join in at familiar places. They had such a lifting effect. One time I remember one of the men read from the Qur'an Surah Qaaf (the chapter called Qaaf). Again, it was beautiful to hear it in that circumstance.

The overall mood was a happy one, despite our bleak immediate outlook. As we approached busy junctions in downtown Cairo, some would start to shout Islamic slogans to the pedestrians and motorists. I started to join in once I understood what was being said. At first we'd shout the *shahada* "*La ilaha illa Allah*" There is no god but Allah, "*Muhammadur Rasool Allah*" and Muhammad is His messenger.

As time went on and our feeling of injustice strengthened, the slogans also become more political, reminding ourselves and others that the one who speaks the word of truth to bring the unjust to account has no shame and should be happy, as Allah does not forget. Occasionally someone would let his anger overcome him as he shouted insults at the president. This was a rare occurrence though.

Sometime later in the prison we were asked to sign a form giving power of attorney to our new lawyer Salah Amin. Then we were allowed to speak to him in the office of the head of detectives in the prison. He was a large serious man in his early fifties. Apparently a well renowned lawyer, certainly well respected. He came with Reza's mother whom we had not yet seen in the prison before. Although not normally allowed, we got to sit for a few minutes with her too. The lawyer explained that he would be appealing our detention, and that he would challenge them to either charge us with a crime, or release us. He told us that the maximum length of time that the law allowed for detention without charging was sixty days. He told us that he had not tried a political case before, but our international links made him stand up to take notice and he was shocked by the overt injustice of it all. Egyptians have grown up hearing of injustices perpetrated against them by their own government, but against a foreigner from the West was truly a new chapter in their history of oppression.

Salah's firm employed an associate lawyer Ulfat, who did most of the liaison work leaving the trial to the big man himself. On our next trip to the Prosecutor we were accompanied by Ulfat when we went into the Prosecutors office. While officially the "investigation" was still being undertaken, in reality our visits to the prosecutor were a mere formality. We were required to visit them every fifteen days. Mostly, after a horrible journey with up to fifty people in the metal van during the July heat, we were left in a holding cell in the basement, then near the end of the day we would be called into the office to ask if we had any requests. Everything was transcribed. On one occasion, I was sent to see an assistant prosecutor (*wakil an-niyabah*), who tried to tease me about my prison conditions. He asked me how the food was, so I replied that it was trash. I asked him if he had ever been inside of the prison? He said no, so I told him that he and his president should spend some time there. By this time I had seen what they can do and was thoroughly fed up with their pretence that this is justice of some kind. Ulfat was laughing after we left the room, as it is not often that people of authority get spoken to in a derogatory manner in Egypt. I was beginning to learn that most of these arrogant fools were so shocked to be spoken to frankly that they didn't know how to respond. Particularly as I was a foreigner, so they couldn't expect the same submission as they did from their own folk.

I soon learnt to have fun with them, at their expense, knowing that all of their bluster and image was just so empty; all the while I could claim to be a foreigner who does not accept or even know of their values and customs.

On another occasion the British Consul Gordon Brown, along with our lawyer, Ulfat, were present in the Chief Prosecutor's office. I stated, on the record, that all of my "confession," extracted from me during the first week was the product of duress, was untruthful and merely the Prosecutor's own words, which I signed under threat of torture. He pretended to be surprised for the Consul's benefit, but soon became annoyed. When I reminded him of how I had requested the British Consul the first time that I had met him, he responded saying that he had called the Consul and that they refused to come saying that they were not interested. I turned to Gordon indicating that he should challenge this statement. To my surprise, Gordon, indicated for me to let the issue drop, so I did. Outside of the room, Gordon said that of course the prosecutor was lying.

Charged

On the fifth of August 2002 three of us were formally charged and so moved from being under investigation to being on remand. This apparently meant that we had more rights now and was a positive sign. It meant that there was going to be some judicial process for us, unlike the thousands of other political prisoners who are interned indefinitely under the emergency laws.

During the night one of the prisoners from inside the cell block had heard on the radio that Hussein was being released and that the remaining three British were being charged. News passed from one window to the next, via the guard then to us. We celebrated Hussein's release. The next morning the Consul visited to tell us what we already knew. Ironically, our case had been brought before a judge the day before, who ordered our release as there were no grounds to continue to hold us, but the prosecutor stepped in to charge us at the last minute so starting the process afresh.

Hussein packed his bag then was taken later that day. We parted with emotion as we had all become fond of each other during those past four months. We later heard that they took him to Alexandria where the State Security tried to pressure him into signing papers against us. They left him in a drowning pool for days and exposed him to some unknown chemicals.

We were now just three, still in the punishment block, but allowed to mix with the rest of the prison population, but still with some restrictions. We had to be followed everywhere by a guard, for example. After about a month more of this, three socialist prisoners had finished their fifteen year sentences and were released, so we were given their cells opposite the punishment block, but crucially, not part of it. We then had relative freedom to live in the prison without a guard following us everywhere. The guards took a while to get used to this situation and continued to harass me and tell me that I was forbidden from such and such. The basic rule in his mind was that as a foreigner I must be forbidden from everything unless he has been told explicitly otherwise. My permission had to be renewed each shift, regardless of the fact the all other prisoners were allowed to do or have the whatever it was that I needed permission for. It became frustrating to live like this, but after two years it had more-or-less disappeared, with only occasional moments of guard paranoia.

The Case Continues

As we were now charged, we no longer had to attend the bi-weekly sessions with the prosecutor. Our first court appearance was due in October, so we had the next two months inside the prison. Our new individual cells meant having a toilet in our cells for the first time, hence being able to use it whenever the need arose rather than planning according to our permitted once per night at 10pm. My cell was in fairly good condition, but the others were a mess. We now had a small garden that the prisoners had made outside of our doors, and new neighbours, Khalid and Muhammad, who each ran the laundry and ironing businesses respectively. Useful neighbours to have who soon became good friends. While in those cells, we would eat together, sharing whatever had been given to us in our visits.

We all were charged with "propagating by speech and writing the ideas of a group set up in contravention of the constitution named Hizb ut-Tahrir which calls for setting up of a Caliphate and rebellion against the government". Maajid and Reza had an additional charge of possessing books for the purpose of propagating the group's idea and Reza had a third charge of "owning a printing device, a computer, for producing literature for propagating the group's idea".

We were warned by our lawyer that we could face a sentence of ten years for the above charges, but our defence would be strong as all the evidence was just books which were bought in Cairo's bookshops and the statements signed by us under threat of more torture.

The case was to be tried in an Emergency State Security High Court and not a military court. This was a mixed blessing. Military courts were totally unjust, with the sentences decided long before the trial. State Security Courts were also unjust, with the judge being obliged to accept whatever the State Security prosecution and witnesses suggested was the case, but they are more visible and so more susceptible to political pressure, whether internal or external. It all meant that there would be a grand show trial with the politicians deciding the outcome. The judge merely controlled the proceedings, but the decision ultimately was not with him.

Our judge was to be Ahmad Izzat al-Ashmawi; notorious as a madman with a passion for handing down harsh sentences. He had recently handed fifteen year sentences to defendants in a case known locally as "*Nawab al-Qurood*" who were accused of financial corruption, taking loans from banks and not repaying the money. Most of whom were in the same prison with us.

They had originally been handed five to seven year sentences, but on appeal were given fifteen years with the judge commenting "If the law allowed me I would have executed all of you". The trial was widely viewed as a show trial to punish individuals who didn't play ball with Mubarak's son's extortion racket.

During this period now that we had been charged, our situation became much the same as the rest of the prisoners. We were harassed by the guards less, left alone to sit with whom we desired, and we started to be entitled to weekly visits. The case was still very much an ongoing matter, so I did not feel safe for my wife to visit Egypt especially as she and our son were threatened as a tool to pressure me while I was in the initial torture facility. She had been living in Egypt with me at the time of my arrest, then left the country a few days later, so I calculated that the risk was too great. My parents, however, were not Muslims, had not been living in Egypt before and were therefore in much less danger from the image conscious State Security police.

My first visit was arranged for September 2002. I started to send letters home asking for photos of my family, an essential, and various luxury items like chocolate, clothes, magazines and books. Seeing my parents and sister for the first time in eight months was not easy, but it was very pleasant.

The prison authorities were not particularly pleasant to my sister, which is out of character for most Egyptians. These were early days, however, so the authorities had not really got to know us yet and were probably still wondering what to do with us.

Egyptians are extremely friendly to all people, but especially to foreigners. One thing that made my father laugh was the insistence on every Egyptian to say "Welcome in Egypt" no matter what the situation. Not only had the grammar tickled him, but also the inappropriateness of saying so when entering a prison. Personally, I had been aware of Egyptian oppression and injustice long before my arrest, so it came as no surprise how I was treated. However, until recently, I feel that most English people are not aware of how unpleasant many of the dictatorial regimes overseas are. They are even less aware of how closely the British government has worked with these regimes over the years. When the reality of life for Egyptians hits us for the first time, it can be a bitter pill to swallow, making it hard to accept. But, when you can see the reality in front of your eyes it can be quite a shock as the sense of helplessness sinks in. It cannot be easy to see your son or brother to be treated in such a way.

In visits and letters I always tried to keep a jolly positive atmosphere, to lighten the mood and to stop any worrying for our condition.

The last thing that anyone wants to hear about their loved ones is details of hardships and suffering. I did not have to hide many details though, as on the most part our general demeanour was happy, due mostly to our outlook on life and the concepts of patience developed through studying Islam.

During the build up to our own trial, our lawyer Salah Amin was taken ill with heart trouble. My parents were visiting me at the time, so visited him in the hospital where he reassured them that he would be fit enough to defend us at the coming trial. A few days later he was dead. It was a shock for us all. Sadly some in the prison saw the comedy of a lawyer dying during a trial and failed to hide their mirth. This only annoyed us, as we were grieving for a man we had put our trust in, while being faced with immature giggling. It led to some tension with a few individuals, but the dust soon settled and things reverted back to normal. This is the way of things inside the prisons. Grudges do get held for a long time, but generally people calm down quickly and don't display such harboured feelings. Living so close together it is in everyone's interest to have a calm atmosphere inside.

The Courtroom

Our first court hearing was quite an ordeal. We were crammed into the same blue steel van as had become familiar by now. Two vans took us on a journey through the hot and busy Cairo streets. We crowded around the tiny windows trying to breathe some fresh air and get a glimpse of the outside world. I was able to see into the distance for the first time in what seemed like ages; although my vision was obscured by the wire mesh over the iron bars. I remember looking out over the city of the dead, a huge graveyard to the South-West of the city. We travelled down the Autostrad road at such a pace, that it made me feel that there was an urgency to bring us to justice, despite all of the procrastination until now. We then turned off of the main road onto a series of unfamiliar back-streets heading towards the centre of the city. Here the jerking stop-start journey began; far more appropriate as an analogy for the pace of the Egyptian judiciary.

Again we sang songs to raise our spirits, but we also chanted political slogans from the windows to turn the heads of passers-by; particularly when we were stalled in traffic. "*mat-khafoosh di-dhalimeen, khafoo bi-rabil 'aalameen*" (Don't be afraid of the oppressors, be afraid of the Lord of the Worlds),
"*la nakhafu lawmata laa-im, al-khilafatu fardun daa-im*" (We don't fear the blame of the blamers, the Caliphate is always an obligation) we bellowed as loudly as we could. We did get some odd looks, although such sights as vans full of prisoners singing Islamic slogans was not an entirely unfamiliar sight in central Cairo.

When we finally arrived at the courthouse '*Dar al-qudaa al-uliyaa*' (The High Court) in the Nasar district of central Cairo, we waited for an hour or more before being led cuffed together in pairs to a back entrance. Just coming out of the van to see, unhindered, the tall buildings and trees was quite a treat. It was odd to see ordinary passers by going about their business, then remembering that just six months ago I was one of them.

There was quite a large media presence at the court's front entrance, so an attempt was made to keep them away from us. We were led to an office with a few chairs where we were kept cuffed for a number of hours. When we left though, we were marched right past them, so were able to make brief comments to the journalists and cameras. We had smuggled paper and pens into the vans with us, expecting to see the world's press; our families in the UK and Egypt had wasted no time contacting them to raise awareness of our situation.

I had written a sign that I held in front of me as I left the van 'Political Scapegoats in Egypt's Suppressing of Peaceful Opposition', as I did not expect to get an opportunity to speak, but I wanted to get my point across, that in this 'war against terror' even peaceful Muslims who called for a just alternative to colonial dictatorships were being targeted, with the implication being that we were guilty of a thought-crime, but that it was OK for the British government to neglect us, as our radical thoughts were part of the terrorism problem anyway. Despite the fact that it was actually British colonial foreign policy that angers so many Muslims, yet us being accused conveniently diverts attention from their wars and support for dictators.

On later occasions when we arrived at the courthouse we were taken in the main entrance, up the steps into the grand marble foyer. We were always handcuffed together in pairs, so we held aloft our Qur'ans as a symbol that we would not be treated as criminals. We wrote banners quoting a verse of the Qur'an "Do you make believers into criminals? What is wrong with you? How do judge?!" As we were led up the steps and slowly proceeded through the foyer we started to sing political and religious songs, as well as continuing our chanting from the van. Soon the officers took to getting us into the courtroom as quickly as possible, embarrassed by the noise that we were making.

On this first and subsequent trips, the accompanying guards were often quite sympathetic to our situation; often unlocking our cuffs when were inside the vans. Even when being marched between van and building, the cuffs were often loose enough that we could remove them at will. Thoughts of running cross your mind, but there would be little chance of getting very far; especially for a foreigner.

Finally we were taken to the courtroom. Here we discovered that number 26 was actually on the run and had not been arrested yet. He was later arrested after we had all been sentenced, including him in absentia. He was re-tried and given the same five year sentence again. Apparently he had turned himself in, as he hated being on the run. The same story I heard from a number of other prisoners who preferred to be inside than outside hiding. The anxiety became too much for them. This is something that I can start to appreciate, as I remember how unpleasant were the nights before a court hearing; being unable to sleep with such an active mind. It made the actual day of the hearing even more arduous as I was now physically exhausted on top of being in such dirty, uncomfortable surroundings. I remember the ease with which I felt when we were taken back into the prison, even when it was for a lengthy pause in the proceedings. At least I knew how my days would be for the coming weeks and months. At least my mind could be at rest.

While defendant No. 26 was on trial, he actually managed to escape, but was re-arrested a few months later after returning to his home neighbourhood. A prisoner from our own prison had been in the van with him on a trip to a Cairo hospital. The guards would be handcuffed to the prisoners while inside the building, except that the escapee had asked to use the bathroom, so the guards waited outside in the corridor. While inside, he had removed the prison white clothes, as he had ordinary clothes underneath, then he left among a crowd of students all leaving the bathroom together. The guards didn't notice him. Our fellow prisoner described the look on the guards faces when they realized what had happened.

Initially we spent the first ten days of our trial in a small cramped courtroom, in a tiny cage to the right hand side. There was a single row of about ten seats and a tiny space for the rest of the defendants to stand. That was bad enough, but we weren't the only occupants. There were already a couple of criminal defendants in the cage when we arrived and more were brought in during the course of the day. There were full bottles of urine and a terrible stench, lingering from the times that prisoners used the floor as a toilet instead. The place was hot and absolutely nauseating.

If that wasn't enough, what I thought was a solid steel mesh around the cage's bars was actually moving. Looking closer I saw that the whole thing was alive with brown cockroaches.

Those first ten days were just to appoint the lawyers, and hear any initial requests. Our lawyers all asked for us to be moved to a larger courtroom and also for us to be allowed toilet breaks throughout the days of the trial. Permission to use the bathroom in twos was granted, but the courtroom remained the same. Over the next two years, the trial was punctuated by various lawyers raising matters of our conditions and treatment. Often the judge did approve such requests.

On one occasion we left the prison doors to enter the van to find all of the other twenty two defendants already inside, each cuffed to his own personal police guard. This was in the midday July heat with fifty men in a tiny steel cage. The guards too were suffering as we were. After a complaint in the court, the judge ordered that we be divided between two vans, with only a small number of guards to accompany us.

Each sitting our own lawyer would make a request that we three British defendants be allowed to make a telephone call to our families at home. Permission was often granted. Initially we were allowed a three minute call in a secure office, with a state security agent struggling to listen to our conversations to record on paper what we were saying. He couldn't really keep up with us though.

After a while, we were left to get on with our calls in peace in the main foyer of the courthouse, with only a minimal force to guard us.

Judge al-Ashmawy was often in hysterical fits of rage during our trial. On one occasion he threw a police guard out of the courtroom for snoring while sitting on a sofa at the back of the room. He also ordered the sofa to *"itla burra!"*, "get out!" was his famous high pitched shriek, such that it became the catchphrase of the whole trial for us. Throwing people out was a daily occurrence. He threw out Yusef, the Egyptian interpreter for the British Consul Gordon Brown, as he was whispering a commentary of what was happening. *"Itla Burra!"* To say he was paranoid is an understatement. On one occasion he thought that something a member of the public was holding was a camera to spy on him, so he ordered an investigation into it. He even put a police officer in the cage with us on one occasion, as his phone had rang while the court was in session.

When the charges were being read to each defendant in turn, the Arab defendants entered not guilty pleas. When Reza was asked he answered that he needs a translator before he can enter a plea. Maajid answered that he also needs a translator, but that he was not guilty. The judge didn't bother asking me, so entered a not-guilty plea on my behalf.

In an early hearing the judge appointed an interpreter to translate what was being said for us three British defendants. He was to sit next to the cage and keep us informed of what was going on. That was until the judge decided that no one should be allowed to talk in court, so told our interpreter to be silent. From then on we had to make do with a brief summary during breaks.

The Prosecution

When the first set of hearings was over, we were ordered to come back after two months to hear the prosecution. This time we were led into a larger courtroom filled with journalists and lawyers.

The cage was larger, but no cleaner. There were about eighteen seats, so with a little rotation we all got a chance to rest during the day. I started to take my prayer mat with me, so I could sit on that as well. There was just about enough room for each of us to pray individually when the time came. Often we were back in the prison in time, so there was no need to do so in such a filthy place. Besides, the toilets were absolutely shocking, so I preferred not to go there unless the need was dire.

One time while returning from the toilet I was greeted by the State Security officer who had actually come to my flat to arrest me. He was due to give evidence as a witness later that day. I briefly reminded him not to lie, to which he responded "I never lie". He went on to tell the court about his arrest of another defendant, who confessed everything to him in the car to the police station. He left a much younger officer to claim that he had arrested me, before I confessed to everything in the car as well.

The judge did question him, after prompting from the lawyers, about what my flat looked like, what floor was it on and so on. The 'witness' could not answer any of the questions. When asked what language I confessed in, he replied 'broken Arabic and English', although when he was asked whether he spoke English, he replied 'no'. Finally, he was unable to explain how I was able to give so many pages of detailed confession during a half hour car journey to the police station.

The judge continued to expose such blatant lies from all of the prosecution witnesses. All of them were State Security officers claiming that each of us had confessed everything freely and voluntarily. The judge became so incensed at the inconsistencies that he ordered the most senior State Security officer to come back the next day to explain why. He was a rosy cheeked, red-nosed man, with the appearance of an alcoholic. For a moment I allowed myself to think that they may actually throw the case out. What that officer actually said, I don't know, but the case continued anyway. Over the two years we came to know the court appointed translator quite well. When all of the prosecution had presented its case he was shocked and told us that he is amazed that the case even exists on such feeble evidence. Even the charges, he said, are not accusing you of doing anything wrong.

Before the trial had got underway, we had complained to the British Consul and our families to the British Foreign Office that the case was based entirely on lies extracted under torture. I had been assured by the head prosecutor in the presence of the British Consul, that the confessions would not be used in court. As it turned out, those confessions and the witnesses who came to say how freely we had given them were the entire basis of the prosecution's evidence against us.

To be absolutely clear about the nature of the trial, one of the lawyers questioned the prosecution as they were reading the charges "are they being charged with any violence?" The prosecutor Waleed al-Minshawi replied that we were not accused of being involved in anything connected to violence or terrorism at all.

We were all actually charged with only 'promoting in speech and writing the aims of a banned organisation Hizb ut-Tahrir, which aims to establish a caliphate.' Reza and Maajid were also charged with owning books of the organisation, while Reza had a third charge of owning a printing device, a computer. There was clearly no real belief that any of us posed a threat to national security, nor that we were at all dangerous. Our only crime was one of thought in a police state that forbade all opposition. For this reason Amnesty International adopted us as prisoners of conscience.

However, both the Egyptian and the British press ran stories when we were first arrested that four British terrorists had been arrested in Cairo. Our families at home complained to the papers, who didn't exactly retract their previous claims, but they just stopped making them in subsequent articles. One thing that we weren't able to get altered was the BBC's obsession with insinuating that Hizb ut-Tahrir had been involved in a coup attempt in 1974 and that it is accused by Egypt of being involved in terrorist activities. This is clearly a false and unsubstantiated allegation. Moreover, it is merely echoing the fanciful excuses of a violent dictator, Hosni Mubarak for his repression. Not even the prosecution in the largest trial against Hizb ut-Tahrir members in Egypt's history accused us of such things. At best it is just lazy journalism and at worst it is aiding a dictator in his oppression. In any case it is certainly not unbiased the journalism that the BBC would like us to believe they stand for.

The matter that took the longest amount of time during the first year of the trial was the large amount of physical evidence presented to the court. When it was first presented the judge discovered that it had been so badly catalogued and disorganised that he ordered it to be corrected then presented again. This accounted for another month's delay.

In any other court in the world, such evidence would be inadmissible, but not in the Egyptian High State Security Court. Such a shambles reinforces the suspicion that this was merely a show trial in a courtroom, but that sentencing decisions were being made elsewhere.

Boxes labeled as having computers and laptops had all gone missing. Books were found for which there was no record of them existing. Even Hussein's British passport appeared as evidence.

I laughed along with the British Consul Gordon when this appeared. Other highly incriminating evidence included children's books. My father wrote in a letter to a Select Committee on Foreign Affairs "These consisted of, inter alia, numerous books in English and Arabic, a sports magazine in English, a passport, a return air ticket to London, a diary recording the development and progress of one of the men's children, and perhaps worst of all a collection of supermarket till receipts—in reality everything consisted of what was grabbed at random by the arresting thugs."

After all of the books were painstakingly recorded in the court record, a defence lawyer requested that they be referred to the Centre of Islamic Research, affiliated with Al-Azhar, to rule whether they contradict Islamic jurisprudence.

He pointed out that some of the books in question are on the curriculum at the Centre for Islamic Studies which is affiliated with the Ministry of Higher Education, for example *Al-Nizam Al-Iqtisadi fil-Islam* (The Economic System in Islam), which is written and adopted by Hizb ut-Tahrir!

The Defence

Our own defence preparations had taken an unusual turn. One day we received a note that our lawyer Salah Amin had been taken ill and was in hospital. Our families paid him a visit, but everyone seemed optimistic that he would recover soon. Then suddenly, we received a visit in which we were told that he had died of a heart attack. Clearly this was a big shock. Reza's family in Cairo had appointed him, as he was considered one of the best lawyers in the country. They had visited another well known lawyer, but didn't warm to him. Salah Amin, on the other hand, had came across as sincere and honest.

After mourning his passing for some time, Ulfat offered to continue to work on our case, but would appoint another more experienced lawyer to prepare and deliver the actual defence arguments. We appointed Dr Magdi Rauf, professor of law at the University of Cairo. We actually only met him on one occasion in a prison visit, in which he took notes to use as a basis for preparing a defence. Conversations with family revealed that he expected us to be found guilty but sentenced to time already served, as it was coming up to two years imprisonment now, hence we would be able to return home soon.

Before the lawyers presented their defence arguments to the judge, the Centre for Islamic Studies report on the books was read out. All books were found to have no contradiction with Islamic jurisprudence or scholarship. Some were recommended to become standard reading material for Egyptians, while a few were recommended to be banned in Egypt, as they could lead to instability. These were the ones that mentioned Hizb ut-Tahrir, or were highly critical of Hosni Mubarak's regime. So, without the lawyers uttering a word in defence, the case against us had unraveled from the prosecution's own evidence.

When the defence lawyers did get to speak it became a bit of a chaotic shambles. There were more than fifteen lawyers all trying to draw the attention of the judge to sometimes obvious contradictions and at other times obscure pieces of law. Most defendants chose their own lawyer to represent them, but one human rights lawyer asked to be allowed to represent the whole group. Another lawyer, Muntassir az-Ziyat, who was famous for defending the Jamat al-Islamiyyah group attempted to appoint himself as our own lawyer. He had earned himself a bit of an unwelcome reputation among the prison population, so we sent a message through the internal prison postal service (smuggled papers and memorised messages) that he should desist, to which he duly did.

On the day scheduled for our lawyer to present our defence he made no appearance, which was slightly worrying at first. The judge ordered an adjournment for some days, which was not at all unusual by now. When the court resumed, our lawyer was now present, which made us feel a lot more relieved.

Specifically related to me, our defence lawyer asked to present receipts proving that I was studying at too basic a level of Arabic to have been the dangerous propagator of thoughts that I was accused of being. Bizarrely the judge refused to allow them to be admitted.

After the first day of the defence lawyers speaking, the prosecutor al-Minshawi requested permission to address the court with a statement. Unusually, he was granted permission to do so. He stood up to say that we were not charged with being members of Hizb ut-Tahrir, so there would be no need to focus the defence on such matters. The defence duly obeyed, or were reminded by the judge that that issue had already be addressed. Ironically, at the end of the trial, and after the judge had decided that the prosecution evidences did not hold water, he himself imposed upon us all the charge of membership.

First Visit

After the defence arguments were over and the prosecution had rested its case, I felt less worried about my wife and son returning to Egypt for a visit. Prior to this the possibility of them being used in some way to put pressure on me was more realistic, whereas now that did not seem to be likely.

We arranged for them to come in September 2003 with my father accompanying them. I had not seen them for over a year and a half now, so of course I was very anxious. On the day of the first visit I was standing by a large iron gate that led into the management block. It was at the far end of a long corridor, with the main door of the prison at the other end. I saw their red passports first, so I knew that they would be coming in soon. Then I saw my tall father and then my wife being led to a desk to deal with some paper work. I then caught sight of my four year old boy holding his mummy's hand looking around bewildered. Amazingly, he saw me standing at the gate so I called out to him. He came trotting across the corridor, guided by a prisoner who worked to assist the visitors. The guard allowed me to open the gate so I went in to hug my son.

He greeted me so sweetly, saying I love you daddy! I nearly melted with a mixture of happiness and sadness. By this time my wife had turned to see us, so we greeted each other, but I was being rushed into the visiting area, away from the corridor.

I took my son in my arms, then he asked me "how did you get out of Egypt? I thought you were stuck there." This is what he had been told since he was two and a half, when one day he could not find me anymore. Saying that I was stuck there was something that he could understand, although I think he imagined me to be stuck in some mud. Each day he would sit by the door wondering if I would return that day. If he saw a white English man, he would ask him "have you seen my daddy?" One time he even asked the window cleaner if he knew where his daddy was.

We sat down together for a few minutes before my wife and father arrived. It was almost as though no time had passed between us. He straight away started to show me his Lego bag, with pockets and toys inside each one. We were to start playing immediately, to make up for lost time, I presume.

When my wife and father arrived we were able to finally see each other for the first time in over a year and a half. My son had become quite popular with my Egyptian prisoner friends, as I would often read them letters about his antics and show them my photos. He was soon whisked away to play with them and be fed biscuits and drinks. I think he liked all of the attention and it gave us adults a chance to speak, for a while. He soon came back, along with all his presents, to resume the Lego game that we had started earlier.

The Sentence

After all of the court proceedings had come to an end, the judge announced a five month adjournment for him to reach a decision before announcing it on 25th December 2003. An interesting choice, as this is a notoriously slow-news day in Britain. In any case, it meant a five month rest from the circus and a chance to return to some routine in the prison. By this time we were in a large group cell with twenty prisoners, while our previous cell blocks were being refurbished.

One evening we heard excited prisoners tell us that a man had attacked Ahmed Mahir, the Egyptian Foreign Minister, in al-Aqsa mosque in al-Quds, Jerusalem. The Egyptian reporter was accusing him of being a member of Hizb ut-Tahrir, so the prisoners were very worried that this would have a negative effect on our sentencing two days later. We later heard that there had been a cultural meeting held by members of Hizb ut-Tahrir in the mosque that day. One of the men listening to the talk had seen the Egyptian delegation enter, so went to loudly accuse him of being a traitor for watching idly as Israel attacked innocent Palestinians. To make his point clearer and to show his absolute disgust, he threw his slipper at the head of Ahmed Mahir, which is a huge insult to such an Arab man.

This same scenario would later be repeated with George Bush in Iraq and Asif Zardari, Pakistan's president, in Birmingham. Throwing shoes at politicians has become the standard expression of disapproval and frustration as people's opposition are silenced. Were it not for the cage I should liked to have thrown my own shoes at the State Security Officers and all those who arrest and accuse innocent Muslims of being criminals, when in reality all they are doing is exposing the oppression and calling to a just system to be applied in the Muslim lands.

In any case, there was some controversy in the prison, as debate raged whether this shoe throwing incident would impact on the way Islamic prisoners were to be treated. The point that I argued was that even if it did, and our sentences were lengthened in revenge, it is not the slipper throwing that should be accused, but the oppressive Egyptian regime that cares only to protect its interests, not those of the people. In the end, the judge announced without any explanation that the sentencing would now be adjourned for another three months, then promptly left the courtroom. The name of Hizb ut-Tahrir had become a talking point on prime time TV and throughout the media, so I assume that they did not want to fuel it more with the conclusion of our trial.

After this incident we started to see serialised and detailed double page articles in newspapers devoted to investigating who Hizb ut-Tahrir was. It was interesting for us to read about how the party had grown in the world while we had been inside. The Lebanese parliament had even declared the party legal, so an office was re-opened there, after years of being forced underground.

Then finally were back taken to our final court hearing. The circus had resumed for the last time. There were many more guards than we had ever seen. A weekly English magazine printed a satirical cartoon once of a demonstration in Cairo; with one demonstrator surrounded by one hundred riot police. It was very apt as it perfectly described what we saw that day as we left the vans.

We could see our families, who had come for the hearing. We could see many well-wishers had come to be part of the crowd. We could see a sea of journalists completely filling the steps of the main court house.

In the court room itself we were able to speak to journalists through the cage. We were left for quite a long time, as the courtroom filled getting busier and busier.

None of our friends and families were allowed into the court room, so they filled the foyer. Most of those filling the seats inside were from the Egyptian and the world's press. For periods we took to singing to create quite a pleasant atmosphere of peaceful resistance to oppression. We wanted all present to be absolutely clear that we were neither ashamed of the accusations against us, nor were we afraid of the consequences.

I remember that just as the judge had asked us to stand to hear our verdict and sentences, Maajid said to me "smile it's your verdict", so we stood cheesily grinning as we were told that we each had five years with labour and a fine to pay. We must have made quite a sight, but the emotions were genuine. Nothing that we could have done would change the verdict at that stage, so it is our belief that this is what has been written for us and decreed. We were not about to become displeased with what Allah has decreed for us, so we resolved to endure all hardships with patient perseverance. This is our basic belief as Muslims and the very reason that we were even being brought to trial.

I looked over to the British Consul and could lip-read him saying "Oh Sh**", which made me laugh. We had developed quite a strange relationship over the past two years. We were often jovial, but at times we had to be quite firm.
Before we left the court room I saw him being mobbed by journalist. In the papers we read that he had said the standard line "the British government does not comment on the outcome of trials... etc."

On the way out of the courtroom, we were led down a corridor of riot police. Perhaps led is too feeble a word, we were pushed and dragged down the corridor, to the back stairs and into the vans. A photo that was published in a paper or website reporting the event shows my collar being grabbed by a guard and me almost choking as I am pushed violently. I remember the incident and also being struck at least once with a baton to make us move along quicker.

I had a TV camera thrust into my face as we turned a corner. I remember making a quick comment that "this proves that Egypt is a land without Islam (*dar al-kufr*), as we were convicted only of calling for Islam." I also remember that one of the prisoners next to me said, half ironically and half annoyed, "do you want another five years?"

When we arrived back at the prison, there was some surprise; more from the guards and officers than the prisoners. Those who worked for the police forces allowed themselves a naivety that somehow they were upholding justice; whereas anyone else who has witnessed the daily injustice has no such illusions, as they know the regime only upholds itself.

Within weeks we were expected to change our clothing to navy blue, as we were now convicts. We were still labeled as political prisoners and kept in the same cells as before, but we were no longer on remand, so the colour changed to signify that. I still kept hold of a lot of my white clothing though, as it was far more suitable for the hot weather. However, in family and Consular visits and any other trips to the management block we were expected to dress in blue.

Life inside the Prison

Life is monotonous in prison. I read Nelson Mandela's autobiography while there, in which he wrote probably the best description of prison life: "The hours seem like years, but the years seem like hours." Daily routines take on a whole new meaning, to the point that some days you have filled your day with so much, that you could not find time to do everything. Regular activities would include exercise, breakfast, walking, reading specific books, teaching English, collecting washing, prayer times, walking with a friend, preparing dinner, visiting a friend etc.

Occasionally, the routine would be put aside. Our fellow prisoners told us that when they were in al-Aqrab prison nearby they had a *rawda* (party) on Eid; where prisoners would sing songs or play games. One prisoner had been to a British school in Cairo, so he new some English songs. They would all sing 'Old McDonald had a farm' with all the farmyard noises. After those prisoners had been transferred into our prison we tried a rendition on Eid ourselves, as we sat together drinking tea after the Eid prayer. Only a few joined in though. They told jokes and amusing stories (usually about Saeedis – southern Egyptian farmers). We even had a real Saeedi to come to talk about his legendary village naivety (looking for the little men in a TV the first time he saw it etc.)
We heard how one Saeedi ate a toothpaste sandwich as he had never seen it before. He had been given the toothpaste by another prisoner as a gift. Of course after 10 years, most of the prisoners had heard all of the stories, but they were new for us.

One day, the brothers from Ikhwan al-Muslimeen (The Muslim Brotherhood) had organised a party in the cell block. It was *nasheed*s, Qur'an, stories, jokes and short sketches. They were all punished for that by the State Security officer as they went on past the time they were supposed to enter their cells.

One night in Ramadan, a different group of Ikhwan brothers organised a party where everyone participated. They brought fresh jokes (having been outside of the prison only a few months before), held competitions and we all ate sweets. It was a very memorable night. One competition was to shout the answer to the following question (in English): "What is the longest word in English?" I shouted out 'Antidisestablishmentarianism' but was told that the answer was 'it's smile' (say it with an Egyptian accent '*Itsa mile*'). The next question was "How do you make oil boil?" to which I said add a 'b' and my friend whom I had taught English to, said add a 'p'. He was awarded the prize to my dismay. The Arabs have a particular problem with the p and b. His prize was only a bar of soap, so I wasn't too upset.

When it was announced that our three-quarter-term release had been approved, the whole cell block and some from the other block held a party for us. Again there was singing, jokes, stories etc. I relayed how in my first year in prison I had attempted to compliment my friend on his strength while lifting concrete weights, so I translated the saying "strong as an Ox", but I didn't know the word for Ox and thought it was very similar to the '*gamoosa*' that I had seen in the village outside Cairo, so I told him that he was strong like a *gamoosa*. He nearly dropped the weight on himself from laughing. Calling someone a *gamoosa* in Egypt is an insult equivalent to calling them a donkey, which is basically saying they are stupid.

My standing joke (after we had read in a newspaper that it had been voted the funniest joke in the UK) was "one duck said to the other quack 'Quack!', so the other replied 'I was just about to say that'" (boom boom). It was universally not understood by the Egyptians, but had all the British and Americans laughing. We played Chinese whispers with it on Eid, but it got stopped half way due to the protests and groans. Egyptian jokes are much more in your face. E.g. the Peugeot joke (Peugeot was a grand car in Egypt during the time that these prisoners entered the system). "Four Saeedis in a Peugeot taxi, the driver driving very fast.

In the back one says 'slow down, I'm scared of your driving' so the driver replied 'Do you know about Peugeots?' the passenger said 'no', so the driver told him to stay quiet then. A little later the other backseat passenger says 'slow down, I'm scared of your driving' so the driver replied 'Do you know about Peugeots?' the passenger said 'no', so the driver told him to stay quiet then. Finally, after more fast driving the front seat passenger says to the driver that he is afraid of his driving, so the driver again asks him is he knows about Peugeots to which the passenger replies 'yes'. The driver then says 'Oh great can you tell me how to slow this thing down?'" This would have most of the Egyptian prisoners in hysterics.

A Muslim Brotherhood prisoner told me a political joke which summarized well the feeling Egyptians had for Mubarak and his supporters. "All of the ruling party heads were playing in a football game which was refereed by Sayed Tantawi, the government appointed Sheikh of al-Azhar. When Mubarak kicked the ball towards the goal, but missed completely, the ref shouted 'Gooooaaal!' so all the others asked 'how?' He replied by quoting a saying of the Prophet 'Verily, the actions are according to the intentions.'" Of course, it is completely out of context, but it is funny because it describes what the sycophants in the regime are prepared to do for it.

Not only the government appointees, though. I once asked a prisoner who had been kept on remand for over 12 years why his father would vote for Mubarak in the presidential elections, as I was shocked when I heard that he had. He explained that his father does not like Mubarak one little bit, but that if he did not vote this way, then he would have no job to go to in the morning.

Finally, while on the topic of corrupt Egyptian politics, I spent some time with a few of the Muslim Brotherhood parliamentarians and candidates. One of them had actually won the seat in Damanhour district, but was told that Mubarak's candidate had in fact won, and then he was put in prison with us. The government man who had supposedly won, however, was forced to flee from the district for fear of being lynched, so hated was he by the people there after his victory was announced.

Dodgy wiring in Egyptian prisons meant that I was regularly shocking myself. I was always fortunate enough that I had thick plastic sandals on at the time, so I never got seriously hurt. One time at night, while we were in the group cells of *amber* (cell block) 3, we were all cooking at about the same time which caused a wire in a junction box in the corridor to get hot and start burning. The electricity cut and the corridor started to fill with smoke.

We first heard the shouts of cell 6 next door to us, then we could smell the smoke ourselves. We had made polythene sheet covers for the barred holes which served as windows, so I tried to close them on the side of the corridor. The smoke started to pour in. From the other window we could see the fire-brigade soldiers so I started to shout '*Nar*' fire. Then some other Egyptian prisoners shouted '*ya MaTafi*' 'O fireman', so they came running with their fire extinguishers. We had to bang on the doors for about 10 or 15 minutes before they agreed to let us out into the smoke filled corridor. The firemen had used powder to put out the burning junction box and part of the plaster on the wall that had caught fire too. After about an hour outside, a fellow prisoner had replaced the burnt out wire, bypassed the melted circuit breakers with more wire and we were all locked back in our cells again to resume our cooking. Nice and safe!

Amber 3 was falling down. When it rained (admittedly only seven days in the year) the roof leaked and some of us got wet. The plaster on the ceiling would fall on our heads. One day it fell on Reza's head on the evening before a British Consul visit. We took the lumps of concrete and plaster in to show them. This may have been one of the factors that led to our eventual move to the newly refurbished cells of *amber* 2. They had been sitting empty for months. We still did not move for about three months from our ceiling complaint, though.

It was just the latest incident after the fire and another in which a less-than-stable prisoner tried to stab an American prisoner at the start of the Iraqi war. He missed and stabbed an Egyptian in the hand who had jumped in to protect the American. Such incidents were very rare, but living on top of each other did sometimes bring out tensions among prisoners.

When we were kept in the cage I could not see further than 20 metres, which actually becomes something you miss. We had bars above our heads, so even though I could see trees, the view was obscured. I tried to climb up to the bars to look through, but I was not very successful. Even when we were let out of the cage, long distances were something I craved. I now had about 120 metres total vision, but this was not relaxing enough for me. One day, a friend showed me how to climb to the top of the minaret in the mosque. We did this in the early afternoon, then I got to see the entire Tora prison complex. What a view that was. I was hurried a bit, so did not spend time savouring it, but it was lovely to see. I got used to the near vision after a while. However, in our final year, we were able to use a weights bench outside; then sometimes in the mornings I could lie there and watch a family of green parrots flying from a distant tree to the water tower and back. These are simple pleasures, but mean a lot to prisoner who has not seen into the distance for years.

Prison History

About a year before we arrived in Mazra'a, most of the political prisoners whom we were about to meet were still in al-Aqrab high security prison, next door. They were all moved in on the morning of September the 11th. The policy of persecution in the Egyptian prisons had just started to change, as the leaders of the largest group 'Jamat al-Islamiyyah' had agreed to a peace and reconciliation initiative with the government. The state security officers had brokered a deal whereby the group's leaders would write books denouncing their terrorism and the use of violence in their struggle, in exchange for the possibility of release and easing of conditions in the prisons. Egypt's other main group 'Jihad' would not see the same until later during the time that we were in prison, however, all prisons did stop the routine beatings at around the same time. After this point beatings and killings continued, but on a lesser scale and were now the exception rather than the rule. Nothing has changed in the state security investigation places even until the end of Mubarak's reign. They still tortured and murdered as many as they ever did. They even killed a few Muslim Brotherhood members while we were inside. One while he was in the cell behind us in 2004.

One day, I had turned a corner near the management block of the prison where I saw one of the criminal worker prisoners on his back with his feet in the air. He was being beaten on the soles of his feet with a cane. The officer tried to smile nervously and pretend that all was OK when he saw me. I was ushered back round the corner.

Most prisoners who died in the prison during our time died due to negligence and a lack of concern for their health by the prison authorities. On a whim diabetic medicine would be refused entry by the prison's governor. Other times it would be allowed. I saw six deaths in our prison. Mostly older men in the criminal wing who were denied proper treatment , a couple of men from our cell block died of Hepatitis C and the one member of Ikhwan who was abused by the state security officers, then left to die in the prison from his injuries the same evening.

I was told that over 350 people had died in Wadi al-Natrone prison while my friend was there for six years. He told me how their cells had slim windows at top, so scorpions could fall in. If bitten then prisoners would have to suck out the poison from the other prisoner's leg. An antidote was available, but not during the night. One time a prisoner had an attack of some kind so the guard was called, he replied that he didn't want to wake the officer. The prisoners called again to say he was dying, but were told to call again when he's dead.
They called to say he had died so the guard should remove the body, but were told to wait until morning.

While we were there, we heard of a scuffle during a visit in another prison, where a prisoner's mother had been insulted by a guard, so the prisoner abused the guard, then was shot. I was told that this had happened many times and the report would mock the incident and would say something like "prisoner died while trying to fight the gun".

When the al-Aqrab prisoners were first allowed visits, it was through a screen in a crowded room for 5 minutes. They were allowed to receive gifts too. Writing equipment was still forbidden, so when one foreign prisoner had arranged for the whole cell block's medicines to be delivered, they arrived at the cells without the papers or packaging. It was anyone's guess who should take what. Some did guess and became ill as a result.

Prisoners had to rely on their ingenuity inside. When the first metal toothpaste tubes were allowed in the cells, prisoners would tear the empty tube into thin strips and attach it to the light socket, thus creating their first heater and were able to boil water for tea. They even made an oven to bake a cake from ground bread and the sugar separated from sunflower seed paste (*halawa*).

Bread, *halawa*, cheese, vegetables, rice, beans and lentils had become more abundant after the start of the new policy. Initially after the peace initiative the prisoners were allowed out of their cells in to the corridor for less than an hour a week, which grew until finally they were allowed out for about eight hours, with some of that time in the sun outside.

I spoke to prisoners who had been inside for twenty years so had seen the situation before the civil war, during it and now afterwards. They had avoided the harshest measures, but not entirely. They still had to endure the generally closed system of the prisons. Before the lockdown they used to spend the summer afternoons pouring water onto their concrete cell roofs and walls in an attempt to reduce the heat inside at night when they'd be locked up. Temperatures inside would regularly reach over fifty degrees centigrade with the crowding and sun. My own individual stone cell, with walls over one metre thick, was a steady 35 to 37 degrees during July and August.

Other prisons, during the lockdown of six years, were allowed visits, but with a catch. On the way back they were severely beaten up.

All prisoners who were not yet convicted of an offence could raise their complaint to a judge every forty-five days. This system was called *tadhallum,* and involved them being transferred back to the police station where they were nominally still being kept in custody. *Tadhalum* for Cairo people meant going to la-Zughli Interior Ministry headquarters, with the Interior Minister in his luxurious office upstairs. In the basement was a dark damp cell. The prisoners would wait there for up to fifty days, then get sent back to prison. They could sometimes see their families though, but had to risk getting sick from the air.

Other police stations were also grim, but often worth the extra suffering just to see loved ones. These trips were the main way for smuggling contraband goods into the prisons, as the police station guards were easier to bribe than the prison ones.

There are many prisons throughout Egypt, although I only saw two of them. Yet, I heard many stories from prisoners who had spent time in the other prisons before being transferred into our own prison.

In southern Egypt in an area called Asyut a friend told me of the daily beatings that all prisoners would receive in Wadi al-Gadeed prison. This was usually administered inside the cell, with sticks, but somewhat half heartedly, to break spirits more than bones.
However, if an officer was made angry by a prisoner, then the guards pulled him out into the corridor and really badly beat him.

Often copies of the Qur'an were forbidden inside the prisons. If a smuggled copy was found it would be confiscated and sometimes a zealous guard may tear it up and flush it down the toilet.

In Wadi al-Gadeed, as the guards came into the cell every day, it was very hard to conceal any contraband items. My friend was fortunate enough to have a *hafiz* (one who has fully memorised the Qur'an) in his cell. Each day he would use the rubber elastic in his shorts to write on the cell wall what they were to memorise that day, then rub out before the next day's inspection / beating. He told me that he would use the time while being beaten, standing hands against the wall, to revise whatever Qur'an he had learnt.

There were normally about fifteen prisoners in a cell with no air in summer, no warmth in winter. Each had less than one 20cm tile width to sleep on. If one moved in the night to use the toilet, then he'd find no room to lie down again when returning. Some prisoners spoke of not having enough room for all to recline at once, so some would stand while others would lie down.

Al-Aqrab prison was populated exclusively by the convicted prisoners (about 500 total in Egypt, out of the 30,000 political prisoners). Each was kept in an individual cell where the door was not opened for six whole years. Food was dropped into their cells through a window in the cell door. It was ten beans a day dropped onto the floor, along with a spoon of rice. They had to rush to eat it before the cockroaches did. The roaches lived in the steel doors and were so hungry themselves that they would eat the prisoners' skin at night while he slept. One friend told me how he had long woken up with bleeding arms, but didn't know what caused it. He had been told that it was the cockroaches, but didn't believe it. Then one night he awoke to find one feeding on his arm.

In our third year in the prison, all other prisoners were transferred back to either Wadi al-Natrone or al-Aqrab prisons. When they came back after seventeen months they showed us their dirty brown water that they had been drinking for the time that they were there. They told us that had a small area of about the size of a basketball court to exercise on for the entire cell block of about 600 prisoners. Things had improved slightly though, as each prisoner now had a hand-span and a half width total to call his own in a cell.

During the harshest times prisoners were still allowed to attend exams (if they raised a case to get a judge to order it) and were allowed their specific curriculum books about three weeks before the exam, but they weren't allowed any pencils or paper. One man had not seen his father for about three years while on remand, although his father didn't know whether he was alive or dead. He was transported to his university for exams heavily guarded. His father had waited outside the gates just to ask a prisoner for news of his son in the prison. He didn't recognise his own son and asked him if he had seen him, to which the son replied "it's me Dad". His father fainted on the spot.

Tensions

With our prison being so predominantly populated by Islamic political prisoners, a lot of the bad behaviour that we hear about from prisons was not a reality for us. We did not have to deal with gangs, drugs, theft, rape, fights etc. The convicts in the criminal wing were generally elderly who had got into a dispute with the ruling elite, or who had a highly placed connection, to secure them their place away from the general rougher criminals. A handful of petty criminals were brought in to serve the rest of the prisoners, working in the kitchens or doing general maintenance work, but they were few in number and never caused any problems.

However, this does not mean that problems did not occur. After a while tensions do build and spill over into something unpleasant.

Oftentimes a scuffle may occur during a football game, but never continued onto anything serious. Once Reza was pursued off the pitch by a young prisoner. A few blows were exchanged before the prisoner announced that he did this to show that he was not weak. I suppose that a misplaced comment or 'tut' at his football skills had been a bit too much that day. They both became friends again the next day. Other prisoners often got involved to calm and settle disputes.

I was often approached by Egyptians asking me to intervene between them and Maajid. Maajid seemed to particularly like attacking the Egyptian's understanding of Islam, so he would challenge them to debate their ideas. The Egyptian's complaint, however, was that Maajid was too aggressive and too relentless in his pursuit. There was little I could do, however, as we had our own tensions to deal with.

I understood the Egyptian's complaint, as I too had been challenged by Maajid to defend my own ideas on occasions. It soon became clear to me, however, that debate was not the way to discuss such matters, as it only ever relied upon who had the best quotes to hand, or who could come up with the wittiest rebuttal. Establishing the truth or falsehood of a stance is not really the focus of the debater; winning and forcing the opposition into submission is all that matters. Anyway, after a few unpleasant experiences, I decided not to oppose Maajid's ideas, as keeping the peace was paramount.

Reza did not share my view for some time, so there were often rows which had started as debates. On one occasion Reza accused Maajid of being an immature tyrant, to which Maajid jumped to his feet, threw his chair across the courtyard and screamed that he could defeat Reza, as he had to defend his manhood after being called a baby. No fight occurred and I then acted as a go-between to keep our relationships civil. From then on, very few debates took place among us, and we just agreed to keep our differences to ourselves.

These tensions were highest after we had been kept locked up for nearly three months after a prison system wide inspection had revealed three mobile phones in a neighbouring prison.

After the Taba bombing in 2005, the State Security went into a frenzy of oppression. They had heard that someone from a city called al-Areesh in North Sinai had been involved, so we heard that they had arrested all men in the city and built a special desert camp to house them. Many of them were then moved into our prison complex. I met a fifteen year old boy, his father, grandfather and uncle, all in the same cell. The Egyptian government had recently set up a human rights monitoring organisation with much fanfare in the press. After a few months of incarceration a few men from al-Areesh in a neighbouring prison had managed to call this organisation using a smuggled mobile phone. They told them that they were being held in Tora prison, so the next day the entire Tora complex was locked down for two weeks of intensive inspections, *tafteesh*.

These inspection days were the worst, as your whole routine was broken and you were looked in your cell. The Faces of the prisoners changed on inspection days, as they remembered the recent past. A *tafteesh* day meant being beaten up and having all of your possessions confiscated.

The basic routine was that your cell would be locked. Everyone would look for places to hide valuables like money, radios, knives etc. The inspecting officers would enter the cell then their soldiers would ransack the place. Any poor or weak prisoner would be abused, while prisoners who looked like they had connections were generally left alone to be inspected by the officers. Most of the stress came from not knowing what you would be left with at the end of the day.

After this particular inspection, all cell-blocks were locked for a few weeks, before gradually the situation returned to normal over the next three months.

Punishment Cells

I was sent to the punishment block during my final summer in prison. My relationship with the State Security officers had been tense in the beginning as I refused to accept my status as a prisoner. I did not respect their orders and restrictions and regularly ignored them. My first year was one in which I was constantly harassed by the guards. I was followed everywhere, forbidden from everything. If other prisoners where all visiting each other's cells, I was forbidden. One time the guard even locked the gate on me to fetch an officer to prove that I had ignored his order to stop. It was an order just for the foreigners, and as I was the most obvious looking foreigner, then I got stopped the most. I didn't exactly blend in with the average Egyptian crowd. Of course the officers were not afraid of us but they were intimidated. We were obviously educated, which is highly regarded in Egypt, along with the fact that we were from Britain, a place that they all dreamed of being in rather than the Egypt of no chances and no opportunity. On top of all of this, they knew that we had three or four Consular visits each year and could make a complaint which would then be taken to their bosses in the ministry. They definitely do not want anyone in the ministry to know their names in a negative context. Egypt is such an authoritarian military state, that each officer is mean to his inferiors as his superiors are mean to him. Rank is everything, even amongst the civilians who all have social ranks.

Our rank as British foreigners was about as high as you can get, just below Americans. Moreover, most Egyptians are Muslim Arab people; regardless of their personal characteristics, they cannot accept for a foreigner to ever have a negative view of their country. We were basically seen as guests and guests must always be treated generously. So I could exploit this extra sway that I had with them, as I knew that they wouldn't ever shout at me, nor punish me except for very serious matters. As long as I was basically in the right and their restriction was obviously whimsical and meaningless, then I could argue my point and then reach a compromise where I would get to go more-or-less where I wanted. I tried to reduce the harassment, but they had their orders to keep it up. It was a silly game, but one that I could work. The officers loved to feel that they had done you a favour, by first denying you something, to make you ask them for it, then they would blame someone else for the ban, reprimand him and allow you it, at which point you would be expected to be grateful, as if he is the real generous guy. One day the state security officer said that we could do anything that we want as long as it doesn't cause him any trouble. Basically, as long as he doesn't get heard of outside. I think that he had given up trying to break us and make us behave towards him as an Egyptian would. I had said to him that we aren't used to your ranking system, so don't expect deferment and respect from me. If you are polite to me them I am polite to you. One time I had told him that he was an oppressor. I had insulted him in front of other prisoners and had spoken to him without any extra groveling that his rank made him expect. This was then the agreement that we had, and it was only slightly revised as his successor and the one after him came to the prison. I had a specific agreement that I was allowed to walk anywhere in the prison grounds without restriction except when a General was visiting; then all prisoners had to enter their cell blocks. I was not to accept any harassment from the guards and was to report any attempt to the officers immediately.

One day, I was walking to the other side of the prison and a guard told me that it was off limits to political prisoners. I could see other political prisoners playing football there and others just walking around so I knew that he was lying. I carried on walking. He then grabbed me, so I turned around and headed towards the management block to report to an officer. I held my hand against him to restrain him as I tried to get past. When I reached the officer, he was a particularly malicious one who just said that he had seen everything (he was in his office so saw nothing) and that I was not allowed to go over there. The next day the officers informed that I had to spend five days in the punishment cell. We negotiated it down to three as I raised an official complaint against the guard and officer.

On the same day, an area supervisor had come to see if he could provoke some political prisoners. He was a very nasty man who was jealous of the State Security's involvement in his prison. There are about six rival police authorities in Egypt all independent of each other and answerable directly to the Interior Minister. This one, Ayman Cici, was from the *Maslahat as-Sujoon* (prison authority) who all hated the State Security's interference with the affairs of the political prisoners. Mazra'a Tora is a mixed political and criminal prison so is one of the main battlefields between these two rivals as they vie for control. This day Ayman came to lock the political prisoners up early knowing that we would complain. He deliberately chose to inform the foreigners (Russians and British) and dual nationals (Dutch and American). This caused one Dutch citizen to lose his temper and start to throw insults at the officer. That was all that he wanted and then left. The next day Hisham, the Dutch man, was informed that he had two weeks to spend in the punishment cells. When they came to implement the punishment the *ma'moor* brought about 10 soldiers, one with handcuffs which he used as knuckledusters to break five of Hisham's ribs. Some of the neighbouring prisoners stepped in to protect Hisham and take him to the cell themselves as a mercy to him. Finally, another prison officer (head detective) Muhammad Tawil kicked Hisham inside the cell breaking another bone. I went into my own cell quietly. Hisham was denied any medical attention for 14 days and eventually spent three weeks in the punishment cell. Finally he had x-rays which showed all of his still broken bones.

During my detention and the harsh treatment of Hisham, Maajid went to the *ma'moor* to protest my detention. The *ma'moor*'s temper had been raised and he said to Maajid "I can have you taken to another prison where the criminals will kill you". He then said in front of a large group of his guards "If I killed you there would be no consequence for me!" Maajid immediately wrote a complaint to the prison authorities demanding an investigation into the *ma'moor*'s conduct and his temporary removal during the investigation. We started a hunger strike, along with one of the Russians, to ensure that the investigation does actually get started.

In light of the violence that the *ma'moor* had just perpetrated against the Dutch citizen, then his public threat to murder a British citizen, it became incumbent upon us to see that he is checked for his excesses. The whole atmosphere inside the prison was rapidly changing and the prisoners where becoming anxious of a return to the bad old days. As our complaint could reach the ministerial level through our contacts with the British and Russian overseas representatives, then we felt that we should act to ensure that it did.

I drank only water during the time in the isolation block and then afterwards during our hunger strike, but surprisingly never felt truly hungry. By the third day I was having dreams of food. I dreamt of cream scones and Heinz spaghetti, not together, of course. I imagined that I'd have a feast when I eventually started to eat again, but when the time came, I was just satisfied with anything, then all of the fantasizing stopped and I had no great cravings for anything in particular. I stopped walking to the mosque after the fourth day, and just sat in bed or on a chair for the rest of the time. I didn't have much energy left.

The prison authorities tried to get us to sign a letter that we were on hunger strike, but to do so would mean that they would put us into the punishment cells until we stopped. We refused to sign. When Maajid's blood pressure went very low, we called on the prison doctor, who then read it, but lied and said it was fine. We had already used our own monitor, which showed 60 over 80. This was the same doctor who was also neglecting Hisham, denying him any treatment for his broken bones.

After nine days the British Consul came to inform us of the investigation's start, so we started to eat again. The *ma'moor* soon went on an unprecedented fifteen day "holiday".

Released

During our stay in the prison we had seen prisoners' sentences finish, yet they remained inside. They would be taken to their home police station, kept there for a couple of months, then returned to us. The official line was that they had to be re-arrested for getting up to their old tricks. The reality was that they had never stepped foot out of the police station. In our own case, all of the twenty five prisoners were still inside, even those who had one and three year sentences. It had now been three years and nine months.

I had seen the leaders of Ikhwan released after three quarters of their five year sentence had passed, but only after a fight in the courts. I was therefore not hopeful that we would be going home soon, nor even that we would leave when our sentence was complete.

Maajid had applied for a transfer to the British prison system to complete his sentence there, although this request was more-or-less ignored by the British authorities. We had seen a British man convicted of drug dealing transferred to the UK, although our case was seen as different, as we were political prisoners and not subject to criminal law or prosecution. I heard later that Maajid had actually written to President Mubarak apologising and asking for a pardon, although that was again totally ignored.
Reza was completely opposed to any request for a prison transfer, and I had not yet made up my mind. It would have made family visits easier, but the conditions would almost certainly be worse than in Egypt.

Anyway, one day we three were called to the *ma'moor's* office. We waited outside for about half an hour, then were sent back to our cells. Later on, we heard that our three-quarter sentence release had been approved. Some documents needed signing, but we were to be released after three years and nine months inside.

It was actually three years and eleven months to the day that we finally flew home. We were taken from the prison to La-zughli interior ministry building near Tahrir square. We were taken to the corridor outside the damp holding cell where we waited for about two hours. Finally, we were led upstairs to an office, blindfolded again and left to sit for sixteen hours until early morning. During the evening the torturers started their work again, taking men who were lined up in the corridor one at a time for their electric shock treatment. While using the bathroom once we met a man whose legs had just been fried, barely able to walk, hysterically crying and trying to clean himself after involuntarily soiling his own clothing.

After this we were taking in a van to the airport, where we spent the rest of the night in the airport's own prison cell, before being escorted under guard all the way to Heathrow.

As we stepped off the plane, two British men led us each to interview rooms. I asked who they were, "MI5 or police?" "A bit of both, we are Special Branch" I was told. We were each asked a number of standard as well as not-so-standard questions. I was asked where I prayed and what I thought of suicide bombers? I told them that it is a crime which I absolutely do not support. "Good, then you will want to keep us informed of anyone in your local mosque whom you are suspicious of, won't you?" Incredulously I replied "you want me to become your spy?" "yes" was the response. I told them that I had read enough spy stories to know that the spy always becomes a slave to the handler and that I did not fancy what they had in store for me once I was no longer of use to them. "OK, then will you be willing for us to visit you sometime soon, then?" I was asked. I replied "If ever I decide to do something like you are suggesting, then I would come to you. So no, do not visit me at home." After this, my finger prints and DNA were recorded and I was made to wait for the others then we were allowed to leave.

I later spoke to Reza and Maajid about their own Heathrow interrogation. They had been asked the same questions as I had. Reza told me that he bluntly told them that they could not visit him at home, while Maajid admitted that he had not thought of a response, so agreed that they could visit him later at home.

As we entered the arrivals hall, all of our families and friends were there to meet us. It was a very emotional moment, seeing your loved ones; some for the first time in over four years.

My son had not been told that I was being released yet, so was at home. I surprised him by knocking on the door. He hugged me, exclaimed "what are you doing here daddy?" then led me upstairs to play with his Lego. He was now six years old.

I collapsed from exhaustion that night, then broke down in tears while praying. I had to rebuild my life again, but I did not know how. *Al-Hamdulillah*, with my family's support, I was able to gradually find my feet and start living again.

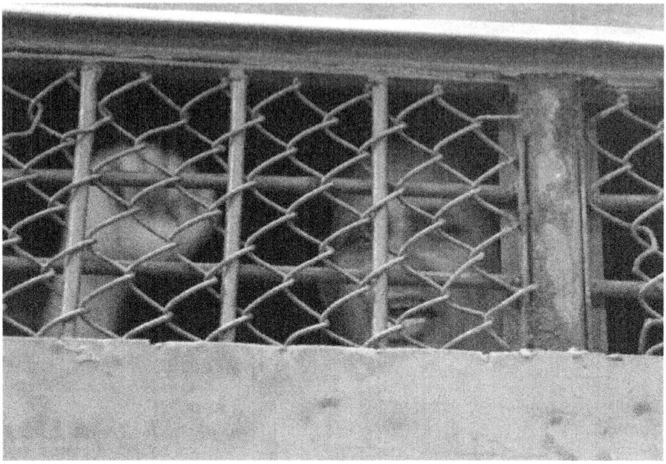

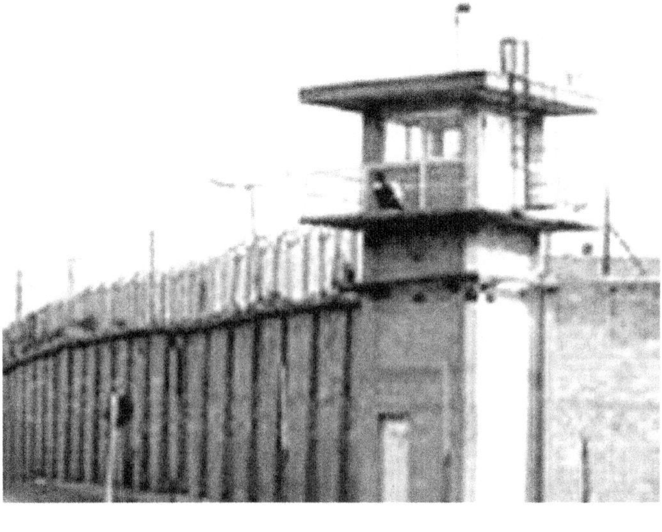

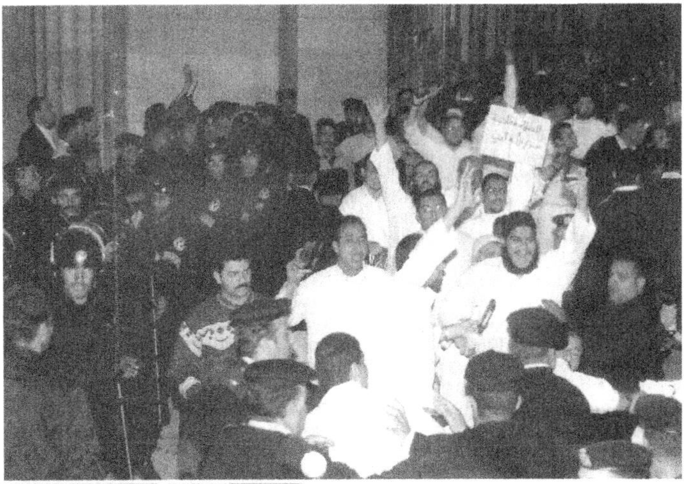

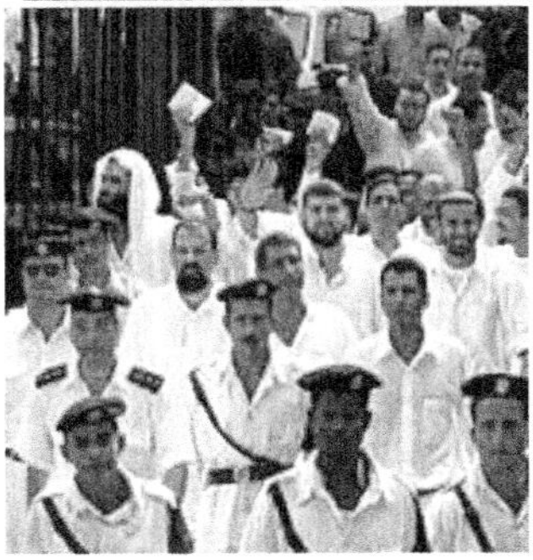

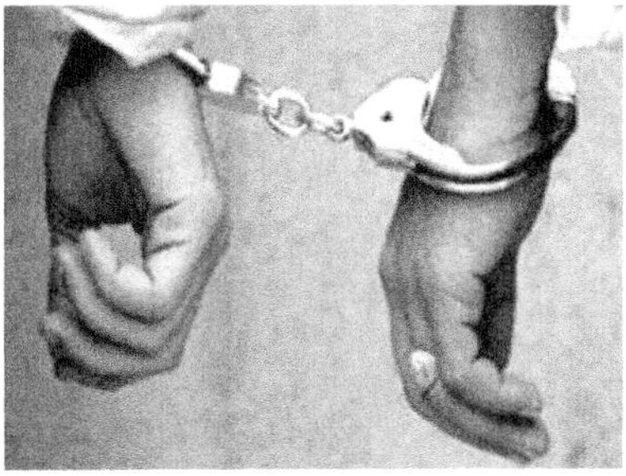

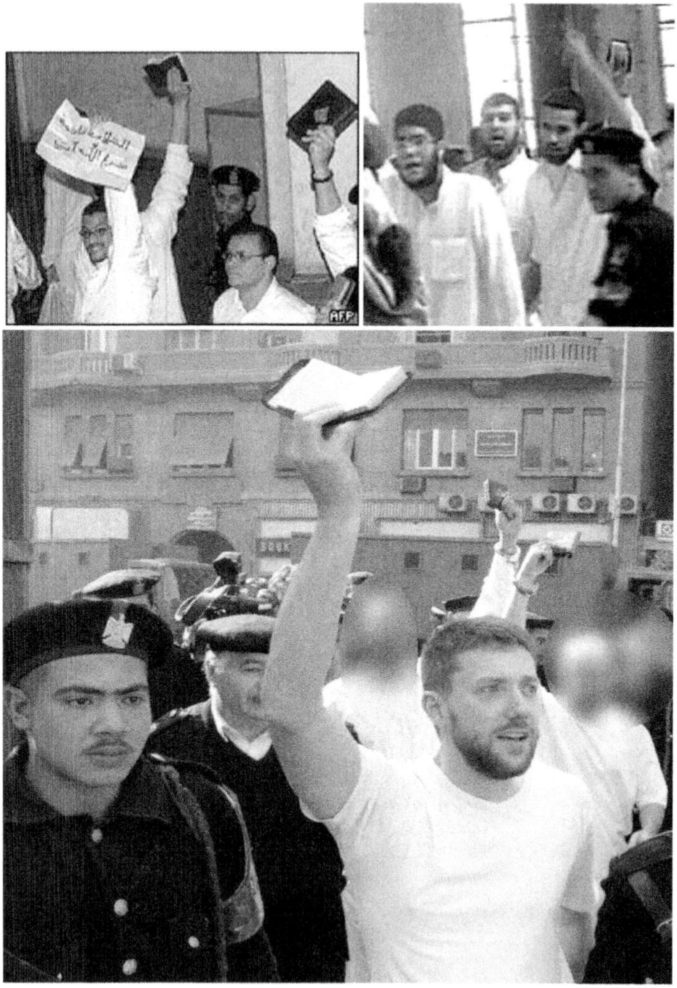

Front door of the prison

Inside the cell block

207

The court house

Arial view of the prison

The blue vans

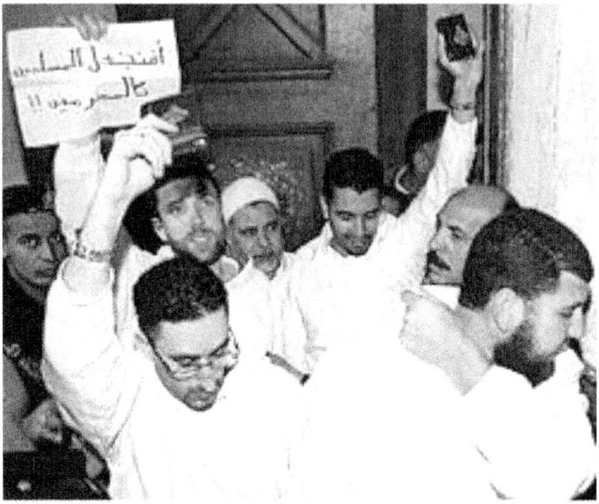

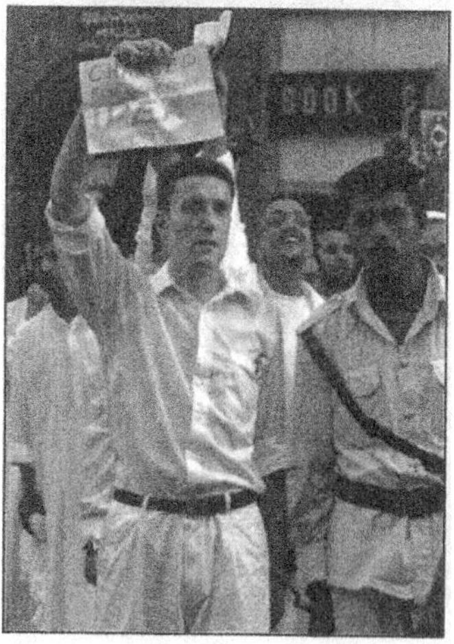
BOOK

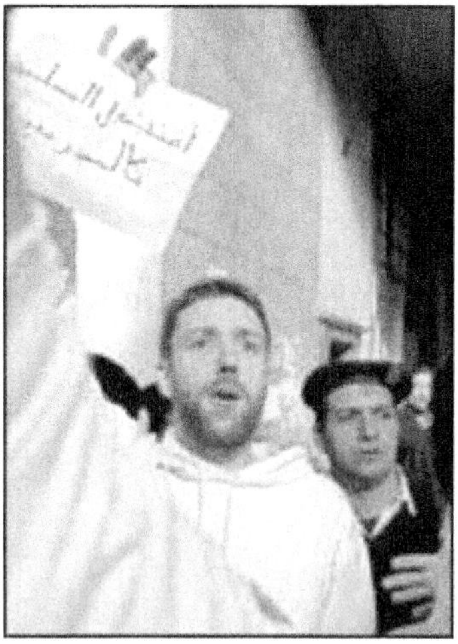

On the way to prison to serve their sentences, defendants of the Liberation Party case chant 'Allah is great'

The courtroom cage

[Handwritten journal page with diagrams]

While ꜤƎ was laughing

Stubborn man
Rasool Allah
Rows of people
me

When we went to the second row to pray

ꜤƎ me

When I started to pray

me
ꜤƎ
ꜤƎ went somewhere else to pray

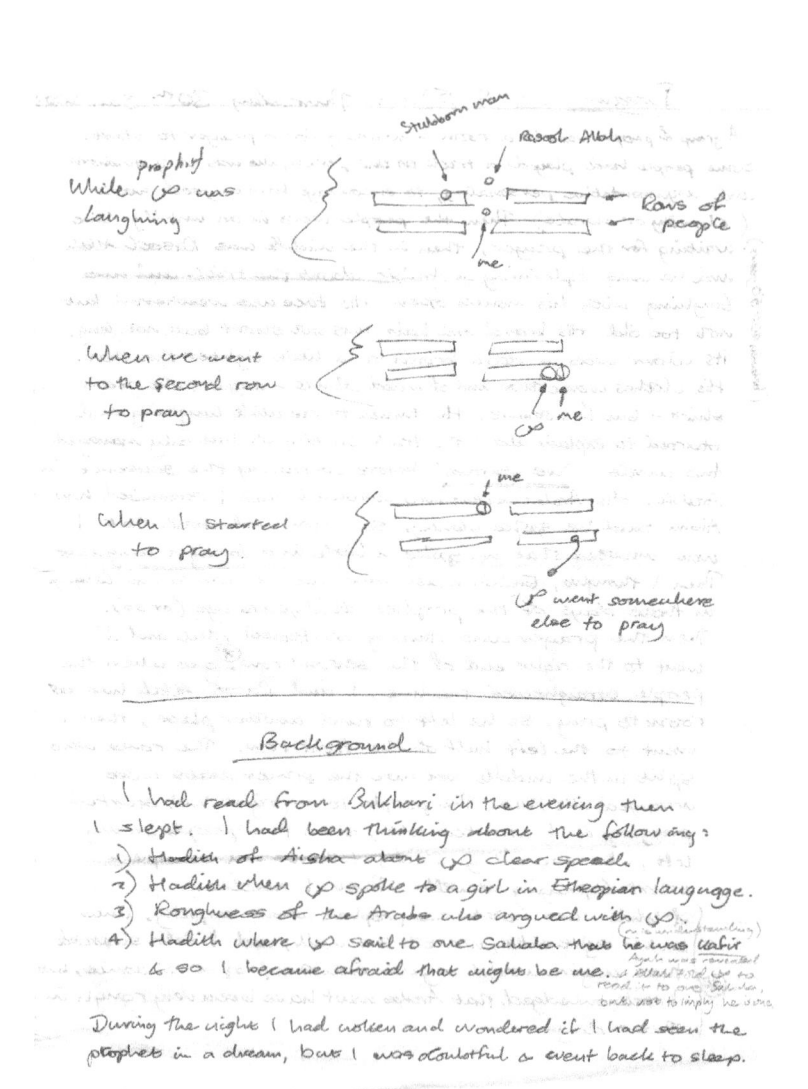

Background

I had read from Bukhari in the evening then I slept. I had been thinking about the following:
1) ~~Hadith of Aisha about~~ ꜤƎ clear speech.
2) Hadith when ꜤƎ spoke to a girl in ~~Ethiopian~~ language.
3) Roughness of the Arabs who argued with ꜤƎ (ꜤƎ smiled/something)
4) Hadith where ꜤƎ said to one Sahaba that he was kafir. Ayah was revealed
& so I became afraid that might be me. telling ꜤƎ not to read it to one Sahaba, ayah was to imply he was

During the night I had woken and wondered if I had ~~seen~~ the ~~prophet~~ in a dream, but I was doubtful & went back to sleep.

I wrote down my dream so as not to forget

Faisal Bodi

Detained in Egypt and ignored here

Blair is doing little to help four British Muslims held without trial

Even as pyrrhic victories go, this week's ruling by a special immigration appeals commission in the cases of nine Muslims held under the Anti-Terrorism, Crime and detained are indeed members of the group but that none of them were in Egypt in an official capacity. Hassan Rizvi, who is not a member, was in Alexandria as part of his Arabic degree at Exeter Univer-

LAWYERS TAKE ON IAN'S CASE

THE case of a former Brackley man being held in an Egyptian jail has been placed in the hands of lawyers.

by Vahsti Hale

Family faces wait for news of man being held in Egyptian jail

Twenty-eight-year-old Ian Nisbet was one of three Britons arrested for allegedly being a member of the Islamic Liberation Party, which is legal in Britain but outlawed in Egypt.

This month his father Alistair, of the Egyptian lawyers."

Ian Nisbet, a former student of Brackley's Magdalen College School, was arrested by armed men in April.

In a letter sent to the British government, he said he was handcuffed and blindfolded for five days and put in solitary confinement since his arrest.

tric shock treatment.

"It is not unusual for people arrested on political charges to be kept in prison for many years."

There is a constitutional ban

Office said they were now waiting for a trial date but added representatives were keeping in touch with relatives of the men.

Mr Nisbet's wife and son are cu

PM's Egypt visit condemned—claim

THE WIFE of a Briton, believed to have links with Tayport and said to have been tortured while on trial in Egypt, has condemned Tony Blair's decision to holiday in the country, according to reports.

Humera Nisbet, who visited her husband Ian in Tora Massra jail, Cairo, criticised the Prime Minister's visit to Egypt, where he is staying with his family.

By holidaying in Egypt, Mrs Nisbet accused Blair of condoning the way her husband has been treated.

Mr Nisbet, whose family is said to be from Tayport, is arrested in April last year and charged with supporting Hizb ut-Tahrir, a banned fundamentalist organisation, and of at

tempting to overthrow the Egyptian government.

Two other Britons—Reza Pankhurst from London and Maajid Nawaz from Westcliff-on-Sea, Essex—were also seized.

Verdicts had been expected last week in the Emergency High State Security Court but the judge adjourned the case until March 25.

It follows claims from the men that they were tortured into signing false confessions they could not read while awaiting the start of their court case in October last year.

They also allege they were subjected to electric shocks and beatings.

Mr Nisbet alleges he was beaten and deprived of food,

sleep and access to a toilet. Mr Pankhurst claims he was subjected to electric shocks for three consecutive nights in an attempt to extract a confession. He also says he was threatened with sexual assault.

In the first few months all three claim they were confined to "punishment" cells measuring just 9 feet by 6 feet with no bed or toilet and allowed out for just an hour each day.

Mr Nisbet's ordeal began in the early hours of April 1 last year when eight policemen armed with rifles, pistols and hand grenades stormed his Cairo home.

He was handcuffed and led away while a computer and other belongings were confiscated.

Last April a letter from Baroness Symons to Nisbet and the other two jailed Britons said there was "reason to believe your confessions were signed under duress."

Hopes the men would be released at a hearing on Thursday, however, were dashed by the court's decision.

Yesterday a spokeswoman for the Foreign Office in London told The Courier the treatment of the men was being investigated.

She had no information on reports that Mr Nisbet's family came from Tayport.

Her information was that all three came from the south east of England, with nothing to connect any of them with Scotland.

Campaign grows for jailed man

by Kerry Hathway
kerry.hathway@ocnltd.com

Group supports bid for men's release

AMNESTY International has adopted a Brackley man as a prisoner of conscience as his father appeals for his release.

Former Brackley resident, Ian Nisbet, 29, Reza Pankhurst, 28 and Maajid Nawaz, 25, and 23 Egyptian men have been adopted as prisoners... Hosni Mubarak within the next two months.

Mr Nisbet's father, Alistair, has pleaded for local people to support a continuing campaign to get the men released by writing letters to the Foreign Office.

He added he had prepared a... Egyptian authorities, calling... the men's release.

The organisation is also ca... for torture allegations to be inv... gated.

For details of the camp... being led by the Bucking...

AMNESTY BACK BID TO FREE IAN

by Vahidi Hido

A BUCKINGHAM group is adding its weight to help free a Brackley man who is being held in an Egyptian jail.

Buckingham Amnesty International will try to help free 28-year-old Ian Nisbet who has been charged for being an alleged member of the Islamic Liberation Party, a group which is legal in Britain but outlawed in Egypt.

John Cornwall, press and publicity officer for Buckingham Amnesty International said: "Our first job is to establish the facts of the allegations and then we will act. We will contact all the other Amnesty groups in the world to add as much pressure as which to the campaign to challenge the Egyptian government."

Mr Nisbet travelled to Cairo with his wife and three-year-old son in October to study Arabic but was arrested by Egyptian officials and has been held prisoner since April.

Two other men were arrested at the same time on the same charges.

Amnesty International is following up reports that the men were tortured with electric shock treatment.

Mr Cornwall said: "This is the first time that we have been involved in a case that is so close to home and we will be giving it our full attention. It is so apparent that he has been imprisoned for belonging to an organisation that is openly peaceful."

Ian's father Alistair contacted Amnesty International to help keep up the pressure for his campaign.

He said: "We still have not heard anything from the Egyptian authorities and are just awaiting a date to be set for his trial. I hope the group can do what they can to help my son."

Buckingham Amnesty International will meet Thursday, September 5, at 7.45pm at the New Inn Buckingham to discuss the campaign. Members of the public are welcome to give their support.

Mr Nisbet, 28, is a former pupil of Magdalen College School in Brackley and was living in London before leaving for Egypt.

● John Cornwall of Buckingham Amnesty International, left, with Alistair Nisbet

'I longed for the basic fatherly duties, such as taking my son to school or reading bedtime stories'

SPECIAL INTERVIEW
by Kerry Hathway

AFTER four long years in an Egyptian prison, unsure what the future might hold, the open arms of family members were an emotional sight for a former Brackley man.

Ian Nisbet, who was freed from prison two weeks ago, is now looking forward to spending time rebuilding relationships with his family, especially his six-year-old

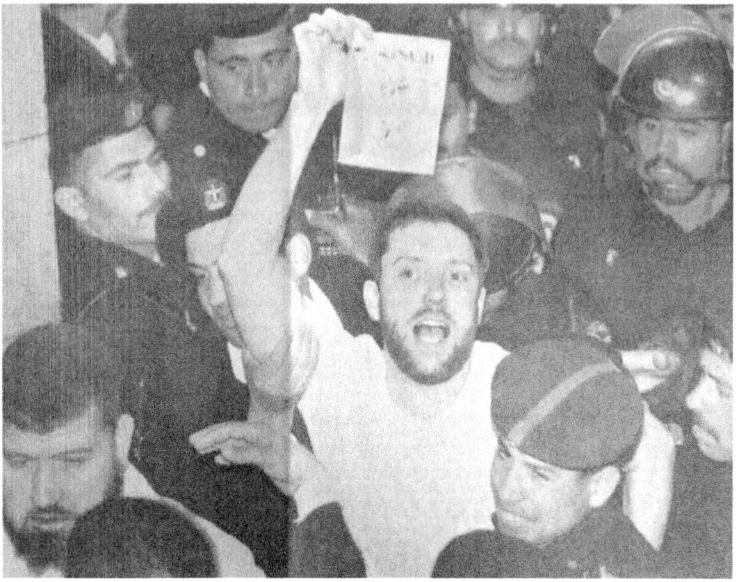

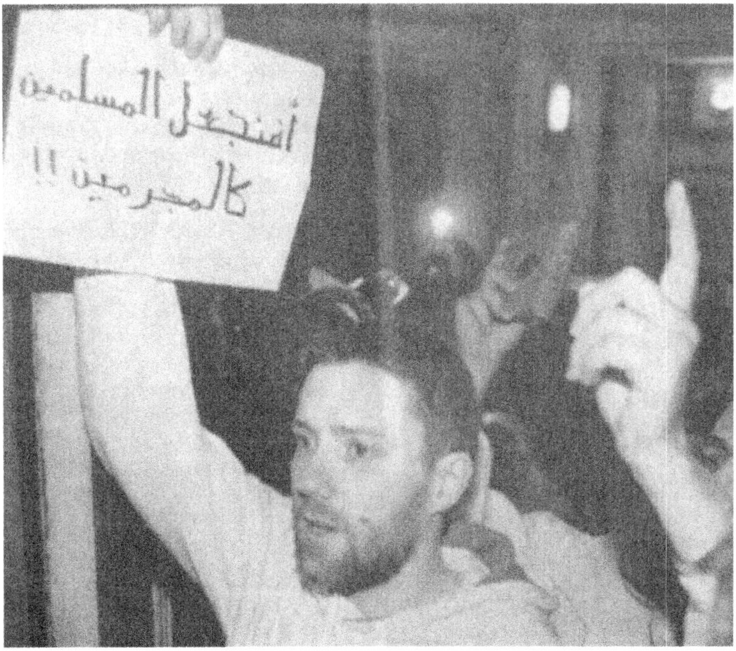
أفنجعل المسلمين
كالمجرمين !!

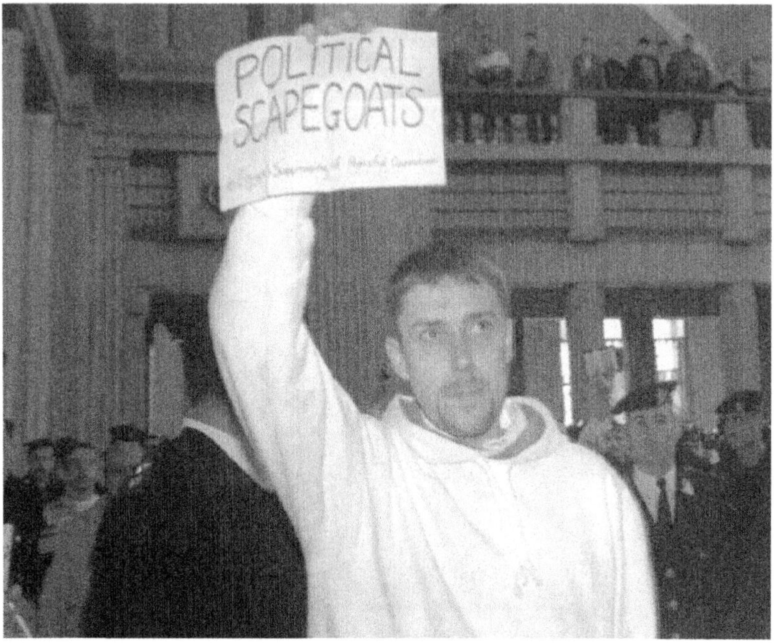
POLITICAL
SCAPEGOATS

Minister backs jailed trio in Egypt

Owen Bowcott

The Foreign Office minister Lady Symons has told three Britons jailed in Egypt for more than a year — allegedly for Islamist views and trying to overthrow the state — that he believes their confessions were extracted "under duress". In an unusually strongly worded statement, the minister responsible for the Middle

Islam, and Mr Pankhurst, 27, are both computer consultants formerly based in London. Mr Nawaz, 24, is an undergraduate at London University's school of oriental and African studies who was attending Alexandria University to study Arabic and law.

The Egyptian authorities claim the trio are active members of the Islamist Hizb ut-

'The worst thing was screaming of victims'

Britons accused of Islamic plot tell of torture by Egyptian police

Owen Bowcott in Cairo

Caged behind metal bars and a security grille in Egypt... man was electrocuted." He has no idea, even now, why they were arrested. "We had at-

---

The Independent
21 Oct 2002
Page: 2

Britons charged with promoting illegal Islamic propaganda 'tortured in prison'

BY ESMAT SALAHEDDIN
in Cairo

the court, they chanted "There is no god but Allah". If found guilty, they face a maximum punishment of 15 years lo[...]

The Guardian
22 Oct 2002
Page: 10

Cairo court refuses bail to accused Britons

Families fear men accused of trying to undermine Egyptian state will be in jail until new year

Owen Bowcott in Cairo

Three Britons arrested in Egypt for allegedly trying to overthrow the state by spreading Islamist views will have to remain in prison until

They have complained they were repeatedly tortured.

"It's very frustrating. Everything is taking so long," said Zara Pankhurst yesterday after delivering food to her son in Masreh-Tora prison outside

by the court: "We are glad, however, the court has now agreed to appoint a translator for the next hearing on October 28. We will continue to press the Egyptian authorities for a response to our request for an investigation into the allegations of torture."

Judge Ahmed Ezzat Al-Ashmawy has ordered the prosecution to make evidence avail-

Daily Mail
21 Oct 2002
Page: 17

'Anguish' of Briton facing 25 years' hard labour

A BRITON facing 25 years' hard labour if convicted of seeking to overthrow the Egyptian government spoke yesterday of his sorrow at his parents' distress.

Ian Nesbit, 28, who is married with a son, went on trial at the Supreme Court in Cairo yesterday.

He and two other Londoners are accused of being members of a fundamentalist Moslem party, the Hizb

Daily Mirror
21 Oct 2002
Page: 4

Held Brits 'tortured'

THREE Britons in court yesterday accused of membership of an extreme Islamic party told how they were tortured as they awaited trial.

IT consultant Reza

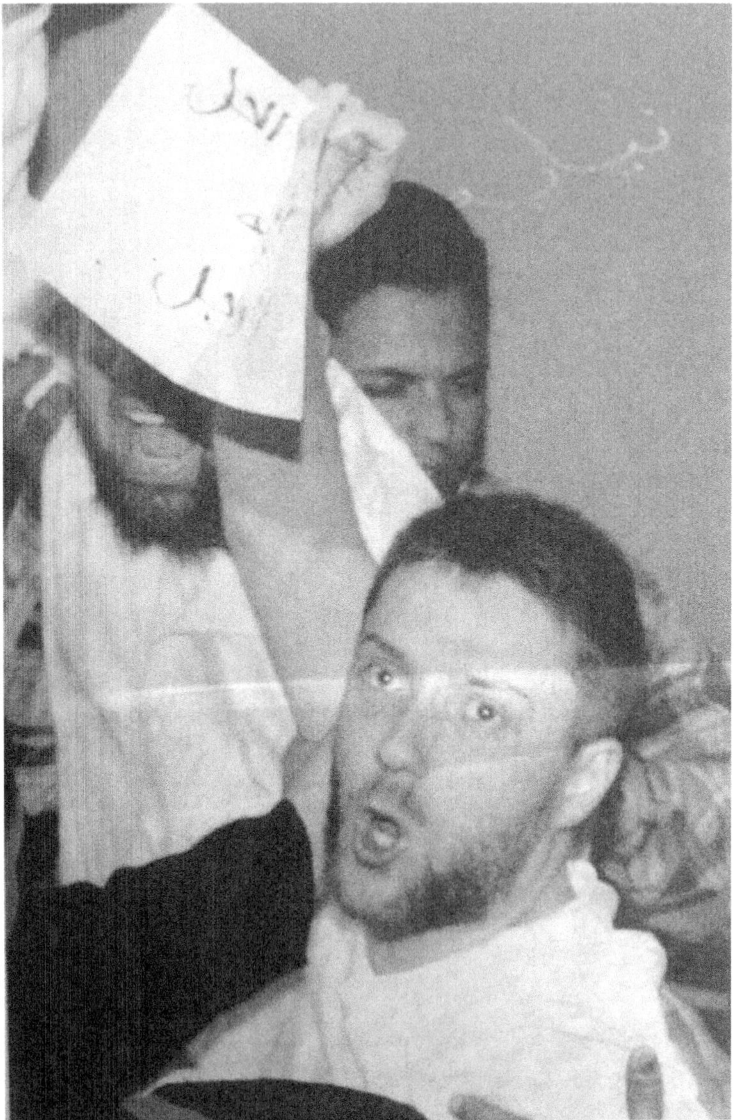

Daily Express
21 Oct 2002
Page: 20

Britons 'tortured in Egyptian jail'

By Jo Willey

ONE of three Britons accused of trying to overthrow the Egyptian government told yesterday how he was given electric shocks, beaten and threatened with sexual abuse in prison.

As a hearing got underway in Cairo, the men told relatives of the torture they endured at the hands of prison officers.

Speaking through the iron grille of the dock in the packed State Security Court in Cairo, deprived of sleep and only allowed to see lawyers after two months behind bars.

IT consultant Reza Pankhurst, 27, Ian Nisbet, 28, and law student Maajid Nawaz, 24, spoke out as they waited for the start of their trial on charges that they belonged to the banned Islamic Liberation Party, known as Hizb ut-Tahrir.

Mr Pankhurst, wearing a prison-issue starched white uniform, said: "I was stripped naked, they beat me, they threatened me with sexual abuse, they tortured me with electricity multiple times, and we were all deprived of sleep."

Mr Pankhurst and Mr Nisbet were working in Egypt with an Internet company and Mr Nawaz was studying at Alexandria University on a foreign exchange programme when they were arrested.

Mr Nisbet said he was blindfolded and

The Guardian
19 Oct 2002
Page: 8

Group says it seeks change without violence

Owen Bowcott

Hizb ut-Tahrir, otherwise known as the Islamic Liberation party, operates legally in Britain but is banned in most of the Middle East and Asia. In Egypt, membership is a crime punishable by a minimum of three years in prison.

Founded in 1953 by Taqiuddin an-Nabhani, a Palestinian graduate of an Egyptian university, it describes itself as a political party whose ideology is Islam and whose aim is to "re-establish the Islamic caliphate in the Islamic world".

under Saddam Hussein."

In Egypt the party has been outlawed since 1974. In parts of central Asia, where it has become a significant opposition force challenging Soviet successor states, its members have been routinely persecuted. The party claims to have 10,000 members in prison in Uzbekistan alone.

The three Britons held in Egypt are all members of the British branch of the organisation. They insist they were not sent to Egypt by the party but moved there for various personal reasons, such as learning

The Guardian
19 Oct 2002
Page: 8

Three British 'torture victims' go on trial in Cairo

Owen Bowcott

Three British Muslims will appear in a Cairo high-security court this weekend accused of attempting to overthrow the state in a trial which threatens to strain relations between Britain and Egypt.

Ian Nisbet, 28, a convert to Islam, Maajid Nawaz, 24, and Reza Pankhurst, 27, all married and from London, say they were tortured by a state security investigations unit to extract confessions.

The men, who were seized from their homes on April 1 and denied access to lawyers for 48 days, have told their families and the British consul they were beaten, blindfolded, given electric shocks and attacks but terrorist charges were dropped.

The foreign secretary, Jack Straw, on a tour to rally Middle East support against Saddam Hussein this month, sought assurances that the Britons would receive a fair trial and pressed for their allegations of torture to be investigated.

Mr Nisbet's parents, who live in Northampton, returned this week from visiting their son in Masreh-Torah and said the ill treatment had stopped. "We had to pay for a mattress for his cell so that he wouldn't sleep on the cold floor," Alistair Nisbet said. "He's got a good attitude. He knows there's no good kicking against the system. His main concern is to get across the injustice of the situation."

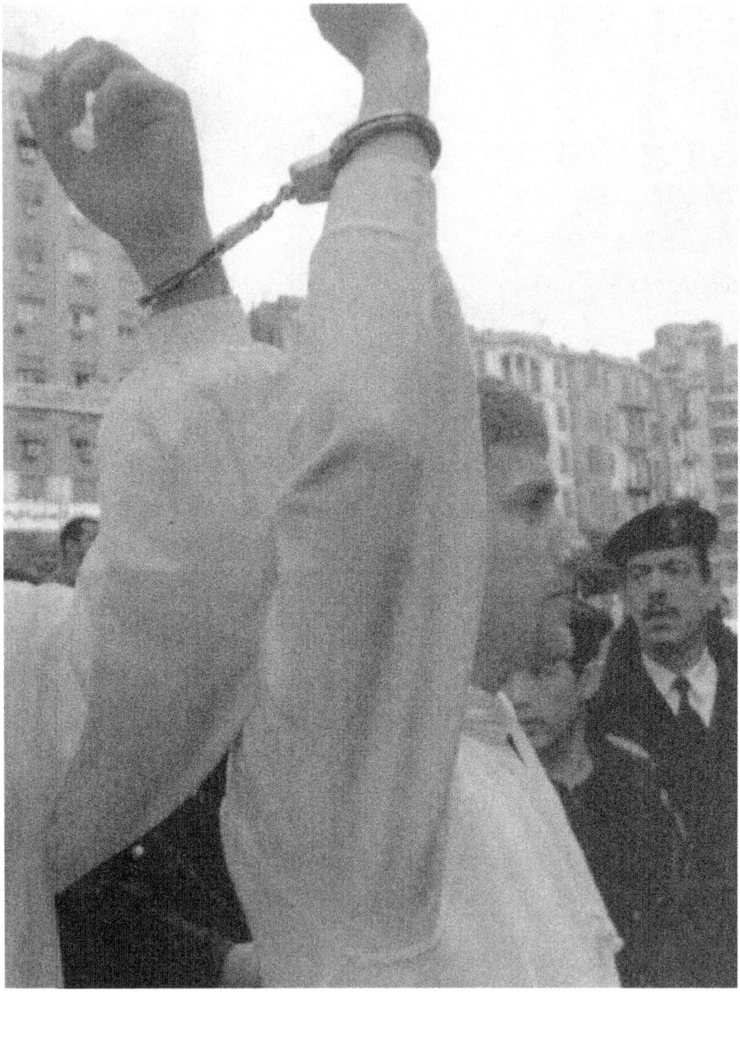

Printed in Great Britain
by Amazon